Better Homes and Gardens®

CHRISTMAS
FROM THE HEART.®

Volume 17

Meredith® Books
Des Moines, Iowa

Better Homes and Gardens.
CHRISTMAS
FROM THE HEART.

Editor: Jessica Saari
Contributing Editor: Carol Field Dahlstrom
Contributing Food Editors: Winifred Moranville, Joyce Trollope
Associate Design Director: Todd Emerson Hanson
Contributing Designer: Angie Haupert Hoogensen
Copy Chief: Doug Kouma
Copy Editor: Kevin Cox
Publishing Operations Manager: Karen Schirm
Edit and Design Production Coordinator: Mary Lee Gavin
Editorial Assistant: Sheri Cord
Book Production Managers: Marjorie J. Schenkelberg,
    Mark Weaver
Contributing Copy Editor: Carol DeMasters
Contributing Proofreaders: Laura DeBoer, Brenna Eldeen,
    Judy Friedman
Contributing Photographers: Dean Tanner/Primary Image,
    Jay Wilde
Contributing Technical Illustrator: Chris Neubauer
    Graphics, Inc.
Contributing Project Designers: Judy Bailey, Darci Borcherling,
    Kristin Detrick, Lynn Jones, Janet Petersma, Ann E. Smith,
    Jan Temeyer
Contributing Recipe Development: Ellen Boeke
Test Kitchen Director: Lynn Blanchard
Test Kitchen Product Supervisor: Jill Moberly
Test Kitchen Culinary Specialists: Marilyn Cornelius, Juliana
    Hale, Maryellyn Krantz, Colleen Weeden, Lori Wilson
Test Kitchen Nutrition Specialists: Elizabeth Burt, R.D., L.D.;
    Laura Marzen, R.D., L.D.

Meredith® Books
Editorial Director: John Riha
Deputy Editor: Jennifer Darling
Managing Editor: Kathleen Armentrout
Brand Manager: Janell Pittman
Group Editor: Jan Miller
Senior Associate Design Director: Mick Schnepf

Director, Marketing and Publicity: Amy Nichols
Executive Director, Sales: Ken Zagor
Director, Operations: George A. Susral
Director, Production: Douglas M. Johnston
Business Director: Janice Croat

Vice President and General Manager, SIM: Jeff Myers

Better Homes and Gardens® Magazine
Editor in Chief: Gayle Goodson Butler
Senior Deputy Editor, Home Design: Oma Blaise Ford
Deputy Editor, Food and Entertaining: Nancy Wall Hopkins

Meredith Publishing Group
President: Jack Griffin
President, *Better Homes and Gardens*®: Andy Sareyan
Vice President, Corporate Solutions: Michael Brownstein
Vice President, Manufacturing: Bruce Heston
Vice President, Consumer Marketing: David Ball
Director, Creative Services: Grover Kirkman
Consumer Product Marketing Director: Steve Swanson
Consumer Product Marketing Manager: Wendy Merical
Business Director: Jim Leonard

Meredith Corporation
Chairman of the Board: William T. Kerr
President and Chief Executive Officer: Stephen M. Lacy

In Memoriam: E.T. Meredith III (1933–2003)

All of us at Meredith. Books are dedicated to providing you
with information and ideas to enhance your home. We welcome
your comments and suggestions. Write to us at: Meredith Books
Editorial Department, 1716 Locust St., Des Moines, IA 50309-
3023. *Christmas from the Heart 2008* is available by mail.
To order editions from past years, call 800/627-5490.

Our seal assures you that every recipe in
Christmas from the Heart 2008 has been tested
in the Better Homes and Gardens. Test Kitchen.
This means that each recipe is practical and
reliable, and meets our high standards of taste
appeal. We guarantee your satisfaction with
this book for as long as you own it.

Better Homes and Gardens®

CHRISTMAS

FROM THE HEART®

contents

Make this special season sugar-sweet with decorating ideas that turn your holiday into a candy land Christmas.

candy land

Sweet as can be, this **Candy Land Christmas Tree,** *opposite,* glistens with goodies that will bring smiles. Popcorn, candy canes, peppermint sticks, glitter-trimmed ornaments, and yards of striped ribbon fill the tree. Dressed in pink and red, the tree holds **Candy Cane Hearts,** *above,* that are topped with a single round peppermint swirl. Turn the page for a close-up look at more ornaments on this holiday candy tree. Instructions are on pages 14-15.

Everyone will look for his or her own special ornament when you make **Glitter Namesake Trims**, *above.* A stripe of white glitter and purchased alphabet stickers make the ornaments easy to make. **Pink Popcorn Treats**, *left,* hang on the tree from a peppermint-stick hanger. Make your own **Peppermint Hot Chocolate Centerpiece**, *opposite,* that also serves as the ingredients for a hot beverage your guests will love. Instructions are on page 15.

Bright and colorful Christmas candies melt together to create **Colorful Candy Trims** and a **Sweet Candy Wreath,** *below.* Use them on a Christmas tree or hang them in a window. Adding more candy coating to a pretty candy cane makes the sweet even sweeter. Give **Candied Candy Canes,** *opposite,* as gifts or arrange them in a festive glass or vase for a holiday centerpiece. Instructions are on page 16.

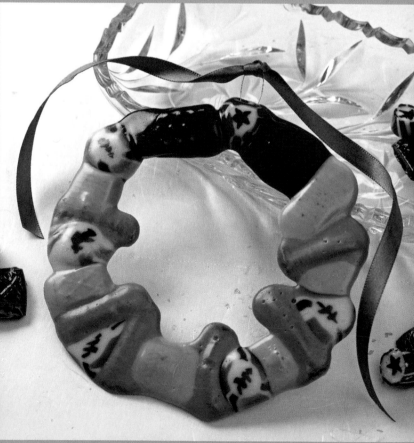

Surround a simple red votive candle with rich red and green ribbon candy to make a **Simple Candy Centerpiece**, *opposite.* Old-fashioned ribbon candies are glued together to make a **Ribbon Candy Card Frame**, *above*, that will accent your favorite greeting card beautifully. Instructions are on page 17.

Candy Cane Hearts

Shown on pages 6–7

WHAT YOU NEED (for one ornament)

Aluminum foil or parchment paper

2 red-and-white or pink-and-white
   candy canes

1 small hard round Christmas candy in
   pink or red

Hot glue gun and glue sticks

10 inches of ¼-inch-wide red or
   white ribbon

HERE'S HOW

1. Cover a surface with foil or parchment
paper. Lay the two candy canes on the
paper to form a heart. Using a small drop
of hot glue, adhere the canes together at
the top and bottom. Add another drop of
glue where the heart forms at the top and
place the small hard candy on top. Let
the heart dry for a few minutes.

2. For the hanger, turn the ornament
over and place a drop of hot glue on the
top of the heart. Fold the ribbon in half
and place on the glue. Let dry.

*Note: Do not eat candy after making
the project.*

Candy Land Christmas Tree

Shown on page 7

WHAT YOU NEED

Christmas tree

White lights

10 yards of 3-inch-wide red-and-white
   striped ribbon

Glitter Namesake Trims

Candy Cane Hearts

Pink Popcorn Treats

Small pieces of ribbon candy (see
   Sources, page 160)

3 yards of ¼-inch wide pink or white
   ribbon

Ornament hooks

3 yards of 1-inch-wide red-and-white
   striped ribbon

Large pink striped candy canes (see
   Sources, page 160)

Purchased pink tree topper

Fine wire

Scissors

HERE'S HOW

After the tree is in the stand, string lights
on the tree. Wrap the tree with the wide
ribbon using it as garland. Put the Glitter
Namesake Trims on the tree using
ornament hooks. Tie the Candy Cane
Hearts on the tree and hang the Pink
Popcorn Treats on the tree using the
candy cane as a hanger. Tie the ribbon
candy on the tree using the narrow
ribbon. Make a bow using the
1-inch-wide ribbon and wire it to the top
of the tree. Hang the large pink candy
canes at the base of the bow. Put the pink
topper on the tree.

Glitter Namesake Trims
Shown on page 7, 8

WHAT YOU NEED (for one ornament)
Purchased pink ball ornament
Double-sided tape
Fine white glitter
Red-glitter alphabet stickers (see
    Sources, page 160)
10 inches of red-and-white
    striped ribbon

HERE'S HOW
Be sure the ball is clean and dry. Cut the double-stick tape into a thin strip. Carefully apply the tape horizontally all around the ball or partially around the ball. Cut two shorter strips of tape. Place one above and one below the strip on the ball, intersecting the stripe vertically. Remove the covering of the tape revealing the sticky surface. Holding the ball over a piece of paper, dust the tape with glitter. Put excess glitter back in bottle. Spell the desired name on the ball using alphabet stickers. Loop a piece of striped ribbon through the hanger and tie a bow.

Pink Popcorn Treats
Shown on page 7, 8

WHAT YOU NEED
18 cups popped popcorn
2 cups sugar
1 cup water
½ cup light-color corn syrup
1 teaspoon vinegar

½ teaspoon salt
1 tablespoon vanilla
Red food coloring
Candy canes
10×10-inch piece of plastic wrap
12-inch piece of red-and-white
    striped ribbon

HERE'S HOW
1. Remove all unpopped kernels from popped popcorn. Put popcorn in a greased 17×12×2-inch baking or roasting pan. Keep popcorn warm in a 300°F oven while making syrup.
2. For syrup mixture butter the sides of a heavy 2-quart saucepan. In saucepan combine sugar, water, corn syrup, vinegar, and salt. Cook and stir over medium-high heat until mixture boils, stirring to dissolve sugar, about 6 minutes. Clip a candy thermometer to the side of pan. Reduce heat to medium; continue boiling at a moderate, steady rate, stirring occasionally, until thermometer registers 250°F on candy thermometer, hard-ball stage, about 20 minutes.
3. Remove saucepan from heat; remove thermometer. Stir in vanilla. Pour syrup mixture over hot popcorn. Add a few drops of red food coloring. Stir gently to coat. Cool until the popcorn mixture can be handled easily. With buttered hands quickly shape the mixture into 2½-inch diameter balls. Place candy cane into ball. Let cool. Wrap each popcorn ball in plastic wrap. Tie a bow on the candy cane where the cane meets the popcorn ball. Makes about 20 popcorn balls.

Peppermint Hot Chocolate Centerpiece
Shown on page 9

WHAT YOU NEED
Red glass bowl or wide mouth vase
Large marshmallows
Peppermint sticks (see Sources,
    page 160)
Prepared hot chocolate
Christmas mugs

HERE'S HOW
Arrange the marshmallows in the bowl or vase. Add the candy sticks randomly among the marshmallows. Use this as a centerpiece. Pour hot chocolate into Christmas mugs and place on the table. Have guests pick from the centerpiece to add marshmallows and peppermint sticks to their mugs of hot chocolate.

Colorful Candy Trims

Shown on page 10

WHAT YOU NEED
Baking sheet; oven
Parchment paper
Christmas hard candies (see Sources, page 160)
Silver dragees
Fine ribbon
Hot glue gun and glue sticks

HERE'S HOW
Cover the baking sheet with parchment paper. Arrange the hard candies on the parchment paper in a tree shape making sure the candies touch each other. Place in the oven at 250°F for about 10 minutes, or until candies have just begun to melt. (Watch carefully—ovens vary and the candies will melt quickly.) Remove the ornament from the oven and press silver dragees where desired to resemble ornaments. Allow to cool. Turn the ornament over and hot-glue ribbon on the back for hanging. Allow to cool.

Note: Do not eat candy used in this project.

Sweet Candy Wreath

Shown on page 10

WHAT YOU NEED
Baking sheet
Parchment paper
Oven
Christmas hard candies (see Sources, page 160)
Hot glue gun and glue sticks
Fine ribbon

HERE'S HOW
1. Cover baking sheet with parchment paper. Arrange the hard candies on parchment paper in a wreath shape making sure the candies touch each other. Place in the oven at 250°F for about 10 minutes or until candies just begin to melt. (Watch carefully—ovens vary and the candies will melt quickly.)
2. Remove the wreath from the oven and allow to cool. Turn the wreath over and hot-glue ribbon on the back for hanging. Allow to cool.

Note: Do not eat candy used in this project.

Candied Candy Canes

Shown on page 11

WHAT YOU NEED
1 cup white chocolate baking pieces
1 teaspoon vegetable shortening
12 candy canes
Decorative sugar, nonpareils, or sprinkles
Small vase or glass

HERE'S HOW
In a saucepan combine 1 cup white chocolate baking pieces and 1 teaspoon shortening. Stir over low heat until melted. (Or combine in a microwave-safe bowl. Microwave on 70 percent power for 1 to 2 minutes or until baking pieces are melted, stirring every 30 seconds.) Transfer melted mixture to a 1-cup glass liquid measuring cup. Dip the bottom or top half of a candy cane into melted mixture, tilting cup to coat candy cane. Immediately sprinkle or roll in decorative sugar, nonpareils, or sprinkles. Let stand for 1 hour or until coating is firm. Makes 12 candy canes. Arrange in small vase or glass.

Simple Candy Centerpiece
Shown on page 12

WHAT YOU NEED
Ribbon candy in desired colors and
    sizes (see Sources, page 160)
Shallow flat glass dish
Votive candle in glass holder

HERE'S HOW
Place votive candle in holder in the
center of the low dish. Surround with
ribbon candies being careful that candy
does not touch candle.

Never leave a burning candle unattended.

Ribbon Candy Card Frame
Shown on page 13

WHAT YOU NEED
Length of ribbon candy in desired color
    (see Sources, page 160)
Aluminum foil
Hot glue gun and glue sticks
White crafts glue; water
Paintbrush
Fine red sugar
Christmas card

HERE'S HOW
Lay the ribbon candy on the foil in the
shape of a frame. Measure the card to be
framed and adjust the candy by breaking
it off to fit the card. Hot glue the corners
of the ribbon candy. Allow to cool. Make
a mixture of 1 tablespoon crafts glue and
1 tablespoon water. Use a paintbrush to
lightly paint the mixture onto the edges
of the candy ribbon. Dust with sugar.
Allow to dry. Glue card to back of
candy frame using crafts glue.

Note: Do not eat candy used in this project.

Use your favorite stitches to sew the happiest of holiday projects this year—for gifts, your tree, and all through the house.

Embroider the words of the season on

a **Christmas Greeting Table Runner,**

above. The runner is made from soft flannel

and the words are couched with decorative

yarns. Stitch your own **Homespun**

Holiday Trims, *opposite,* using cotton

prints with torn edges for a country look.

The instructions and patterns for all of

the projects are on pages 28–30.

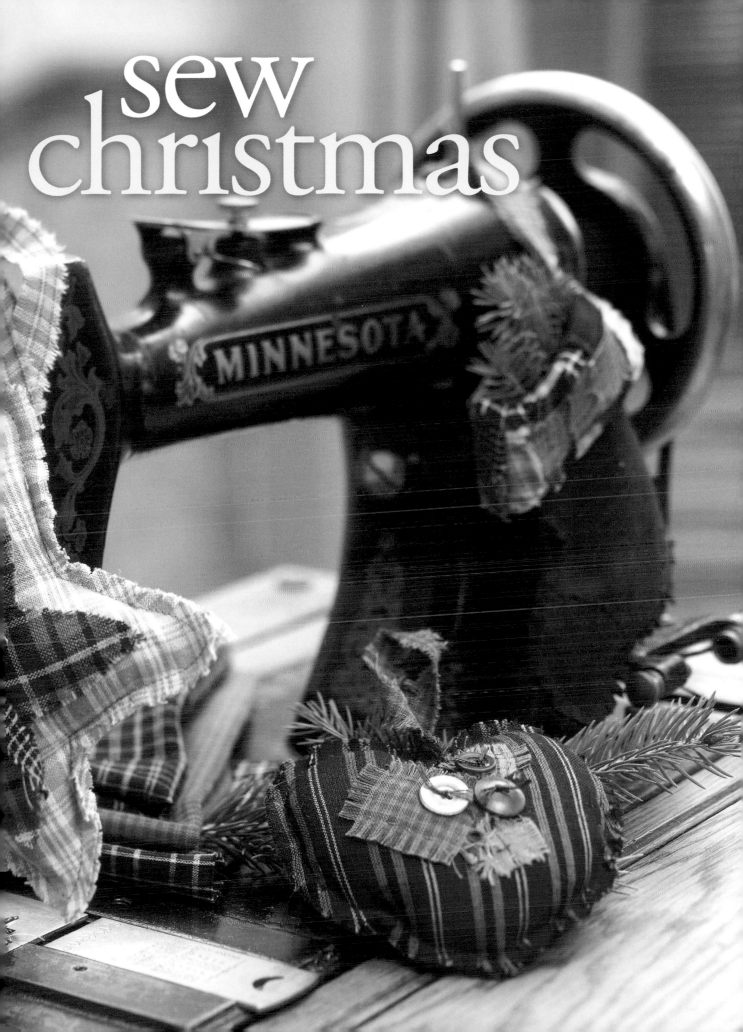

sew christmas

Make a pair of **Pretty Plaid Pillows,** *left* and *above,* by weaving strips of some favorite fabrics in the colors of the season. **Country Christmas Stockings,** *opposite,* are stitched in no time with seams on the outsides of the stockings. The instructions and patterns for both projects are on pages 31–32.

For a colorful and playful table, make a **Quilted Candy Cane Table Topper,** *opposite,* using printed cottons in bright holiday colors. Add a little flair to your tabletop with **Silverware Pocket Placemats,** *above* and *right,* that you make yourself. The simple pockets are stitched to the placemats to hold the silverware. Easy-to-sew napkins complete the setting. Instructions and patterns for these projects are on pages 32–34.

Create old-world charm by making **Woolen Christmas Stockings,** *opposite*, to hang on the mantel this year. The wool is felted and made into stocking shapes. Small wool motifs are appliquéd to the stockings with decorative embroidery stitches. Instructions and patterns for making the stockings are on pages 34–35. Tips for felting wool are on page 160.

Stitch some **Clever Star Coasters**, *opposite*, that take on two looks.

Used flat in bright colors they are pretty stars, or stack them in red to

make a layered poinsettia! Have fun creating your own pattern for

Crazy-Quilted Mitten Trims, *above*, that are stitched using pretty

scraps. The mittens can serve as ornaments or gift holders. Instructions

and patterns for all of the projects are on pages 35–37.

**Christmas Greeting
Table Runner**
Shown on page 18

WHAT YOU NEED

Tracing paper
Pencil
Scissors
Water soluble marking pen
Two 8½×12-inch pieces white
    felted wool
One 8½×8½-inch piece yellow
    felted wool
¾ yard Christmas print
    flannel
63 inches red
    decorative yarn
16 inches green
    decorative yarn
Ivory embroidery floss
Scrap heavy weight
    fusible webbing
Assorted decorative threads
    (found in fabric, scrapbooking,
    and crafts stores)
Matching threads

HERE'S HOW

1. Trace desired word patterns, *right*, and place behind white wool. Mark letters with water soluble marking pen. Couch decorative threads over lettering by placing thread over markings and sewing small machine zigzag stitches over them. Use matching sewing threads for an invisible look.

2. From printed flannel fabric, cut three 2½-inch-wide strips across the width of the fabric. Cut strips into the following lengths: two 32¼×2½-inch strips and two 12⅝×2½-inch-strips. Cut backing piece of flannel to 12½×36½ inches.

3. Use ¼-inch seam allowances to join all fabric pieces. With right sides together, sew white wool pieces onto either side of yellow wool piece across the 8½-inch sides. Press seams open. Using two strands embroidery floss, sew decorative fly embroidery stitch over seam lines of yellow and white wool pieces. Sew long 32¼-inch flannel strips to sides of wool pieces. Sew 12⅝-inch flannel pieces to

bottom edges. With right sides together, sew backing to front, leaving an opening for turning. Clip corners and turn right side out. Press edges flat. With small hand stitches, slip stitch opening closed.

4. On front of runner, lay red decorative yarn over seam line at long edges of flannel. Stitch in place using matching thread and a small machine zigzag stitch. At ends of runner, attach decorative

Faith
Joy
Hope
Peace
Happiness
Love

**CHRISTMAS
GREETING
TABLE RUNNER**
Full-Size Patterns

green yarn in the same manner, sewing through backing at the same time. Using matching ivory sewing thread, straight stitch through the center of the hand embroidery stitches to stabilize through the backing fabric.

5. Fuse webbing to back of selected motifs from flannel fabric. Iron in place in center of yellow wool fabric. If heavy weight webbing is used, no stitches are needed around edges of motifs.

Homespun Holiday Trims
Shown on pages 18–19

WHAT YOU NEED
Tracing paper
Pencil; scissors
Scraps of cotton homespun fabrics
Matching threads
Buttons to trim
Embroidery floss for embellishment
Small pieces of polyester
    fiberfill stuffing
Scraps of lightweight iron-on interfacing

HERE'S HOW
For Mitten Homespun Ornament
Enlarge and trace mitten pattern, *page 30*, onto tracing paper and set aside. Tear strips of cotton fabrics in widths of ½ to 1 inch and weave over a scrap of lightweight interfacing to form a 5×7-inch piece. Iron woven strips to interfacing. Cut mitten pattern from woven piece and another from cotton fabric. Sew ¼ inch from top straight edge

of woven mitten front to stabilize top and tack down woven fabric edges. With wrong sides together, pin mitten front to back. Tear a strip of fabric ½ inch wide and 6 inches long for the hanging loop. Insert loop into side seam at top long edge of mitten and sew front to back, using a ¼-inch seam. Clip outside seam every ¼ inch around outside sewn edges.

For Stocking Homespun Ornament
Enlarge and trace stocking pattern, *page 30*, onto tracing paper and set aside. Tear strips of cotton fabrics in widths of ½ to 1 inch and weave over a scrap of lightweight interfacing to form a 2½×9-inch piece. Iron woven strips to interfacing. Cut two stocking cuff pieces from woven fabric. Cut two stocking pieces from cotton scraps. Tear a strip of fabric ½×6 inches for the hanging loop. On stocking front piece, mark lines for heel and toe stitching. Using 3 strands of embroidery floss, sew over lines with small running stitches. With right sides together, sew side edges of cuff together. Turn and press seams open. With wrong sides together, stitch stocking side and lower edges, using a ¼-inch seam allowance. At side edge, lay hanging loop inside stocking, keeping top raw edges together. Insert cuff inside stocking, having right side of cuff to wrong side of stocking. Sew around top edge using a ¼-inch seam. Turn cuff to outside.

For Bell Homespun Ornament
Enlarge and trace bell pattern, *page 30*, onto tracing paper. Cut two bell pattern pieces from cotton fabric scraps. Tear a strip of fabric ½×13 inches for the woven band. Cut this in half to make two 6½-inch lengths. Tear a strip of fabric ¾×5½ inches and tie a double knot in the end of this strip for the bell ringer. In the front piece of fabric, mark and cut small ½-inch-long slits. Weave fabric in and out of slits and tie bow in center. Tear a strip of fabric ½×6 inches for the hanging loop. With wrong sides together, place front to back. Fold loop in half and insert raw ends between fabric front and back at top center. Place bell ringer strip of fabric between front and back at bottom edge. Sew around outside edges, using a ¼-inch seam allowance, leaving an opening to stuff. Insert small pieces of polyester fiberfill to lightly stuff. Sew remaining opening closed. Clip around outside edges every ¼ inch just to seam line.

For Star Homespun Ornament
Enlarge and trace star pattern, *page 30*, onto tracing paper. Cut two large star shapes from cotton scraps. Cut one smaller star shape from coordinating cotton fabric. Tear a piece of cotton fabric ½ ×6 inches for hanging loop. Tear a piece of cotton fabric into a ⅜-inch-wide strip and tie into a small bow. Trim ends. Sew small star fabric to center of star front fabric, using a hand running stitch about ¼ inch inside cut edges. With wrong sides together, place star shapes together. Insert hanging loop

at one star point, between layers of fabric. Sew front to back using a ¼-inch seam allowance, leaving an opening for stuffing. Insert small pieces of fiberfill to lightly stuff. Sew opening closed. Sew bow to center of star, stitching through all layers of fabric and fiberfill. Clip around outside edges every ¼ inch just to seam line.

For Heart Homespun Ornament
Enlarge and trace heart pattern, *right*, onto tracing paper. Cut heart shapes. Tear a piece of cotton fabric ½×6 inches for hanging loop. Cut 3 small squares of coordinating fabrics for center patches. Pull threads from all sides of the patches to fray outside edges. Sew patches to front, using a small hand running stitch. Sew buttons to heart front, knotting threads and leaving thread tails on top of buttons. Put wrong sides of fabric together and insert hanging loop between layers at top center point. Sew front to back in a ¼-inch seam allowance, leaving an opening for stuffing. Insert small pieces of fiberfill to lightly stuff. Sew remaining opening closed. Clip around outside edges every ¼ inch just to seam line.

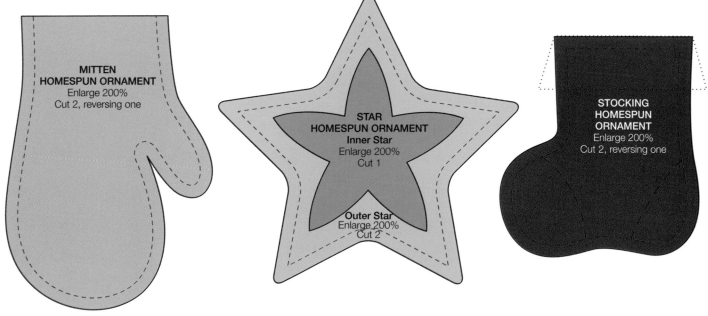

FRONT OF PILLOW

BACK OF PILLOW

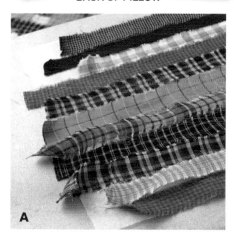

A

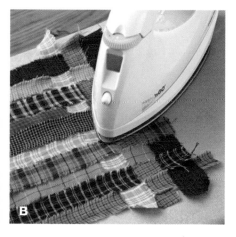

B

Pretty Plaid Pillows
Shown on page 20

WHAT YOU NEED

Scraps of plaid or striped homespun
   cotton fabrics for weaving pillow top
   (about 18 inches long)
½ yard plaid fabric for pillow backings
1 yard lightweight iron-on interfacing
Scissors; matching thread
Three 1-inch buttons for each pillow
14-inch pillow form
12-inch pillow form

HERE'S HOW

1. Tear strips of homespun fabrics to make
assorted widths of ½ inch to 2 inches and
about 18 inches long (12-inch pillow uses
½-inch to 1-inch-wide strips; 14-inch pillow
uses strips up to 2 inches wide). Iron strips
flat, to avoid curling and raveling when
torn. Cut interfacing 2 inches longer and
wider than finished pillow size. Working
on flat ironing surface, lay strips of fabric
across iron-on side of interfacing (see
Photo A). Cover entire interfacing
square. Use additional fabric strips to fill
in lengthwise, weaving them over and
under each crosswise strip of fabric. After
weaving two rows, lightly iron over strips
to adhere to interfacing and keep in place
(see Photo B). Continue weaving strips
until entire square is filled in, ironing
every couple of rows as you weave. Trim
square to 1 inch larger than finished
pillow size. Machine baste ¼ inch from
raw edges to keep all loose ends in place.
2. To make overlapping pillow backing,
cut two pieces of plaid fabric (15×12 inches
for the 14-inch pillow; 13×10 inches for
the 12-inch pillow). Cut 2 strips of
interfacing 1½ inches×length of pillow
top. Fuse interfacing to back edge of plaid
fabric ¼ inch in from cut edge. Fold edge
to back ¼ inch and press. Fold edge to
inside again, another 1½ inch and press.
Stitch close to pressed edge about 1⅜ inch
from side folded edge. These will form the
reinforced edges for the buttonholes and
overlap flap. Make 3 buttonholes in one
piece. Overlap the two pieces, mark
placement and sew buttons in place.
With right sides together, stitch pillow
top to backing pieces, using ½-inch seam
allowance. Clip corners diagonally.
Turn and press. Insert pillow form.

Country Christmas Stockings
Shown on page 21

WHAT YOU NEED

Tracing paper
Pencil
Scissors
¾ yard cotton fabric for each stocking
⅛ yard cotton fabric for each cuff
Assorted fabric scraps for other
   stocking details
Embroidery floss
Matching thread
Decorative buttons, if desired
Scrap of lightweight iron-on interfacing

HERE'S HOW

1. Enlarge and trace patterns, *page 32*.
For each stocking, cut 2 main stocking
pieces from cotton fabrics. Decorate
stocking fronts, as desired. Place sock and
heel pieces in position on top of stocking
front and sew on with a primitive straight
stitch over cut edges, or attach with a
running stitch just inside frayed edges.

Use three strands embroidery floss for decorative stitching. Fray patches on gold stocking by pulling threads on edges of squares and sew with a running stitch using matching thread. Sew decorative buttons over patches. After decorating stocking fronts, sew front to back with wrong sides together, using a ⅜-inch seam allowance.

For primitive stitched cuff
Cut two cuff pieces from cotton fabric. With right sides together, sew bottom seam. With right sides together, fold cuff in half and sew side seam, using ½-inch seam allowance. Turn right side out and press. Using 3 strands black embroidery floss, sew straight stitches over bottom edge of cuff.

For frayed cuff
1. Cut only 1 cuff piece from cotton fabric. Fold lengthwise and with right sides together, sew side seam, using ½-inch seam allowance. Turn and press. Fray bottom edge by pulling threads to desired length of fringe. For ribbon tie, tear strip of fabric ¾ inch wide by 38 inches long. Cut an even number of ½-inch long slits in cuff fabric (this one has 22), cutting 2 inches from bottom edge. Weave torn strip of fabric from center of cuff front around cuff and back to center. Tie in bow, trim, and fray bottom edge.
2. To attach cuff to stocking, tear 1×10-inch strips of fabric for hanging loops. Fold in half and hang inside stockings, keeping cut edges even at top side edges. Place cuff inside stocking, with right side of cuff next to wrong side of stocking and over the hanging loop. Stitch around top edge, using ½-inch seam allowance, also sewing through the loop. Turn cuff to outside and press.
3. Finish stockings by clipping outside seam lines to fray edges. Clip every ¼ inch just to the stitching line all around outside edges.

Quilted Candy Cane Table Topper
Shown on page 22

Finished quilt size: 23½×33¾ inches

WHAT YOU NEED
Tracing paper
Pencil
Scissors
84 squares assorted Christmas cotton print fabrics, cut into 2½-inch squares
4 pieces red cotton fabric cut to 4½-inch squares
½ yard diagonally-printed striped cotton fabric
For inner sashings cut: eight 1×4½-inch strips; two 1×15½-inch strips

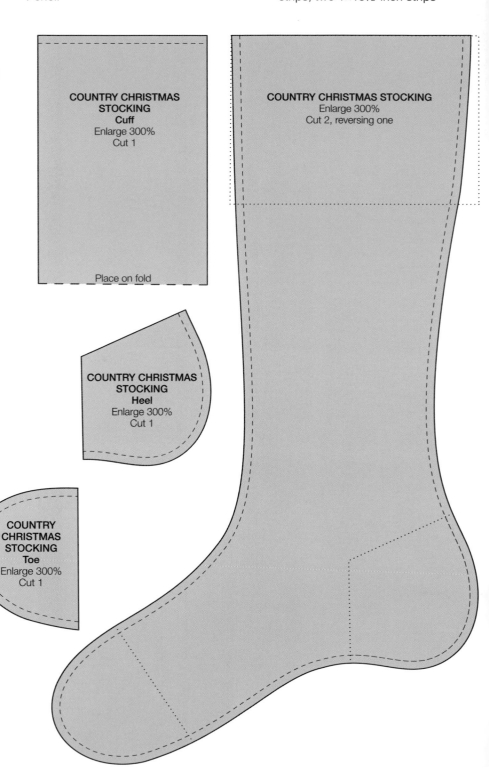

COUNTRY CHRISTMAS STOCKING
Cuff
Enlarge 300%
Cut 1

Place on fold

COUNTRY CHRISTMAS STOCKING
Enlarge 300%
Cut 2, reversing one

COUNTRY CHRISTMAS STOCKING
Heel
Enlarge 300%
Cut 1

COUNTRY CHRISTMAS STOCKING
Toe
Enlarge 300%
Cut 1

HERE'S HOW

1. Enlarge and trace patterns, *below*. Cut out pieces from print and striped fabric.
2. Using ¼-inch seams for all piecing, sew together 2½-inch squares to make a rectangle 7 rows×12 rows. Sew 1×24½ inch striped sashing pieces to each side. Sew 1×15½-inch striped sashing pieces to top and bottom edges.
3. Appliqué candy cane, holly leaves, bows, and berries onto light colored outer border pieces, using fusible webbing; zigzag stitch around pieces. Sew 1×4½-inch striped sashing strips to each end of appliqué border pieces. Sew red 4½-inch squares to ends of shorter appliqué borders. Sew double candy cane appliquéd pieces to center pieced squares. Stitch top and bottom strips to ends to complete top.
4. Layer backing, batting, and quilt top. Quilt as desired. Join together binding strips, fold in half with wrong sides together and stitch to front side of quilt. Hand stitch binding to back of quilt.

For outer binding cut 3 strips
    2⅜ inches×width of fabric
Remaining striped fabric is used for
    candy cane appliqué shapes
¼ yard light-colored cotton fabric
For outer borders cut: two 4½×24½-
    inch strips; two 4½×14½-inch strips
⅛ yard teal blue cotton fabric for
    appliqué bows
⅛ yard green cotton fabric for appliqué
    holly leaves
¾ yard cotton fabric for backing
Fusible webbing to appliqué
25×35-inch piece thin cotton batting
Matching colors embroidery threads
Quilting thread
Sewing thread

Silverware Pocket Placemats
Shown on page 23

WHAT YOU NEED

½ yard cotton fabric for each placemat
12-16 inch square of cotton fabric
    for each napkin
Scrap of coordinating fabric for
    each pocket
12-inch-long ribbon for each
18×13-inch piece of thin cotton batting
Matching thread
Scissors

HERE'S HOW FOR NAPKINS

Napkins can be made in any desired size square. Standard sizes are 12, 14, and 16 inches squares. Cut napkin square to desired finished size plus 1 inch all around to allow for hemming. Press under all edges ¼ inch. Press that edge under again. To miter corners, trim across outside corners diagonally, cutting only half the corner. Press the new corner down diagonally to the inside press line.

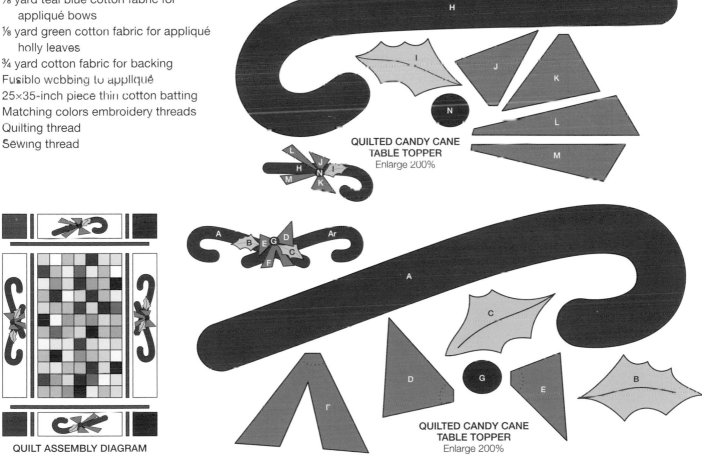

QUILTED CANDY CANE TABLE TOPPER
Enlarge 200%

QUILTED CANDY CANE TABLE TOPPER
Enlarge 200%

QUILT ASSEMBLY DIAGRAM

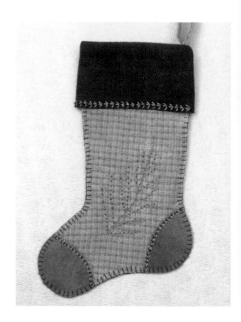

about 1 inch from bottom and side edges of placemat's cut edges. Topstitch pocket to placemat top, sewing close to side and lower edges and reinforcing at start and finish of stitching.

3. Place right sides of placemat fabric together. Put batting layer behind these two layers. Pin 3 layers together around outside edges. Sew together using ½-inch seams, leaving an opening for turning. Clip around corners, turn, and press, pressing in open edges the same ½ inch. Topstitch around outside edges, stitching ¼ inch in from outside folded edges.

Woolen Christmas Stockings
Shown on pages 24–25

WHAT YOU NEED
Tracing paper; pencil
Scissors
Two 9×15-inch pieces felted wool for each stocking body (see page 160 for tips on felting wool)
Two 4×7½-inch pieces felted wool for each cuff
Assorted felted wool scraps for other stocking details
Embroidery floss; matching thread
Note: Decorative stitch diagrams are on page 160.

HERE'S HOW
1. Enlarge and trace patterns, *opposite*. For each stocking, cut 2 main pieces from wool. Decorate stocking fronts as desired. Appliqué wool pieces onto front of stocking with small hand buttonhole stitches around outside edges, stem stitch inside holly leaves, and fern stitch for evergreen bough on gold stocking. Toe and heel pieces are laid in position on top of stocking fronts and sewn on with decorative hand stitches. Green stocking heel and toe pieces are attached with the buttonhole stitch; gold stocking pieces with a fern stitch with French knot in the centers; red stocking has closed buttonhole stitches. At lower edges of cuffs, sew decorative stitches. Use 3 strands embroidery floss for decorative stitching. After decorating stocking fronts, sew front to back with right sides together, using buttonhole stitch and 3 strands embroidery floss.

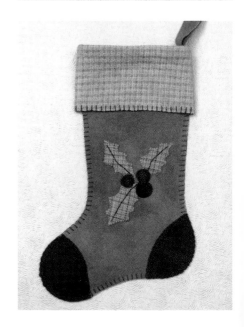

Repress the first press of the edges. Press edges under again, making corner meet diagonally in center of the corner. Topstitch the hem into place, pivoting the material at the corners.

HERE'S HOW FOR PLACEMATS
1. For each placemat, cut 2 pieces of fabric to 18×13 inches. Cut cotton batting to same size. Determine the pocket size desired (for square package, cut a 5-inch square; for rectangle, cut a 4×6-inch shape) and cut 2 from coordinating scrap of fabric.
2. Prepare pocket by placing right sides together and sewing a ⅜-inch seam line around side and lower edges. Clip corners diagonally, turn and press. Fold in the open edges ⅜ inch and press. This will be the bottom of the pocket. Cut ribbon lengths to fit across and down the pocket, leaving ¼ inch to fold around to the back. Pin ribbon at top edge of pocket and sew over ribbon through pocket fabric. Position pocket onto lower edge of place mat top, placing folded edges

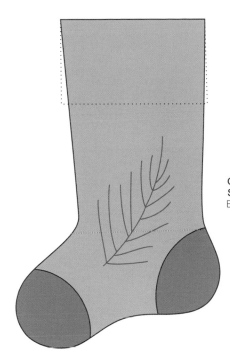

WOOLEN CHRISTMAS STOCKINGS
Enlarge 400%

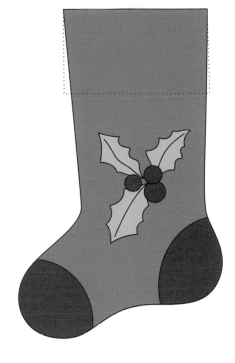

2. To attach cuff to stocking, cut 1×8-inch strips of fabric for hanging loops. Fold in half and hang inside stockings, keeping cut edges even at top side edges. Place cuff inside stocking, with right side of cuff next to wrong side of stocking and over the hanging loop. Stitch around top edge, using ⅜-inch seam allowance, also sewing through the loop. Turn cuff to outside and press.

Clever Star Coasters
Shown on page 26

WHAT YOU NEED
Tracing paper
Pencil

Scissors
Fabric scraps
Star pattern
Thin cotton batting scraps

Matching thread
Metallic sewing thread
Metallic embroidery thread
Needle

POINSETTIA COASTER
Enlarge 200%

STAR COASTER
Enlarge 200%

HERE'S HOW

1. Enlarge and trace star pattern, *above*. For each coaster, place fabric right sides together and cut two star patterns. Place cotton batting scrap behind layered fabric shapes, placing behind one fabric piece's wrong side. Sew layers together in a ¼-inch seam line, leaving an opening along one whole straight side of a star point for turning. Trim batting close to stitching line and across seam at points. Turn star right sides out and press flat. Whip stitch opening closed with matching thread.

2. *For star coasters,* sew spiral quilting design onto center of star shapes. *For poinsettia coasters,* sew leaf vein quilting design onto center of star points. Satin stitch centers using 3 strands metallic embroidery floss. Stack finished shapes.

Crazy-Quilted Mitten Trims

Shown on page 27

WHAT YOU NEED

Tracing paper; pencil; scissors
Scraps of blue colored fleece or
 velour fabrics
Scrap blue velour fabric for backs
Scrap blue satin fabric for linings
Scrap muslin for fronts
11 inches of ⅜-inch-wide blue
 grosgrain ribbon
Assorted colors of blue
 embroidery floss
Blue metallic blending filament
 for embroidery
Matching sewing thread

HERE'S HOW

1. Trace full-size mitten pattern, *below*. Cut 2 mitten pieces from pattern for linings, 2 for backs and 2 from muslin to piece the mitten fronts. With right sides together, sew lining pieces together around side and lower edges, using a ¼-inch seam allowance.

2. Trace mitten pattern onto muslin and reverse pattern for other mitten, marking lines for piecing on muslin. Using numbering sequence noted, sew blue velour fabrics onto the muslin using a paper piecing method of working on the back side of the muslin and sewing right onto the lines marked on the right side of the muslin. Using 2 strands of embroidery floss and 1 strand of metallic blending filament, sew decorative stitches along seam lines. Using one strand of metallic blending filament only, sew snowflake designs on front patches. Sew stocking front to back in ¼-inch seam allowance. Clip curves and turn.

3. Cut ribbon in half to make two 5½-inch pieces for hanging loops. Fold loop in half and baste to top edge of mitten, having raw edges even. Place mittens inside lining pieces, having right sides together. Stitch around top edges with a ¼-inch seam allowance, keeping an opening in the back to turn. Pull mitten through opening and work the lining back inside the mitten. Pin opening closed and hand sew together using matching thread. Press lightly.

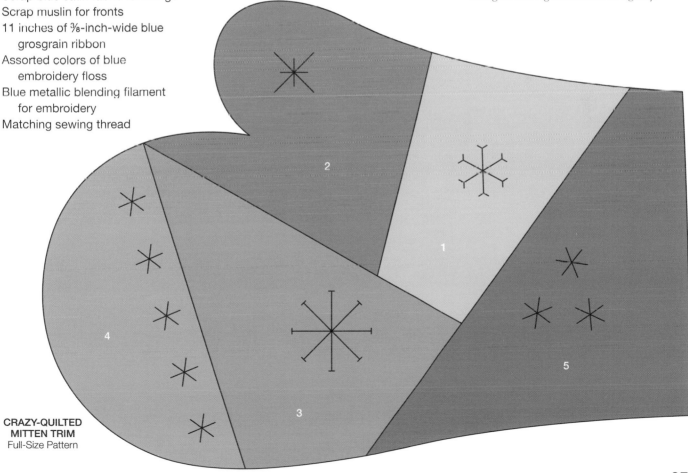

**CRAZY-QUILTED
MITTEN TRIM**
Full-Size Pattern

happy &
bright holiday

Bring some excitement and sparkle to your holiday with happy and bright projects for every room of the house.

Count down to Christmas with this **Happy Advent Calendar,** *opposite,* made using a cookie sheet for the base. Simple magnets hold the clever daily pieces of your handmade art using all kinds of scrapbooking embellishments. Instructions and ideas for the decorated days of the month are on page 48.

Chipboard is a good choice for **Baby's First Christmas Album**, *left*, *above*, and *opposite*, because it is reminiscent of children's board books and allows for lots of creativity. Add favorite embellishments and a dear poem along with adorable photos of baby. Instructions and the poem are on pages 48–49.

Brighten up your holiday with clever **Mirrored Christmas Shapes,** *above* and *right,* to use on your tree or anywhere in your home. Then make a matching **Mirrored Christmas Stocking,** *opposite,* using your favorite colors of felt. Patterns and instructions are on pages 49–51.

Winter

came down to our home one night
Quietly pirouetting in on
silvery-toed slippers of snow,
And we, we were children once again.

Bill Morgan, Jr

Display a favorite holiday quote or saying with this sentimental **Snowflake Message Frame,** *above,* using a purchased frame and mat. Just add the embellishments and message you want to send. Make giving a gift card extra special by designing your own **Bright Gift Card Tin,** *opposite left.* **Paper Gift Card Holders,** *opposite above right, and below,* can hold gift cards too. Craft them in a style to fit the lucky ones on your list. Instructions for all of the projects are on pages 52–54.

Argyle Gift Card Holder, closed

Argyle Gift Card Holder, open

Bright Gift Card Tin

Folding Gift Card Holder, open

Folding Gift Card Holder, closed

Flowered
Gift Card Holder

Entertaining

- [ ] Plan holiday party: theme, menu, and décor
- [ ] Send invitations
- [ ] Purchase supplies for party
- [ ] Clean house, prepare food
- [ ] Host holiday party
- [ ] Clean up and put away decorations

Christmas Cards

Recipient / Sender

Year:

Gratitude is the memory of the heart.

Jean Baptiste Massieu

Thank You's

Christmas magic world, and beholds everything is softer and more beautiful.

~Norman Vincent Peale

I will honor Christmas in my heart, and try to keep it all the year.

Charles Dickens

Decorate a small lunch box to create a **Clever Christmas Organizer,** *above* and *opposite*. Keep track of everything you need to do to get ready for Christmas—sending Christmas cards, decorating, buying gifts, entertaining, baking, and writing thank-you notes. Instructions are on pages 54–55.

Happy Advent Calendar

Shown on pages 38–39

WHAT YOU NEED

Cookie sheet (not nonstick coating
    variety)
Spray primer
Acrylic paint in desired color
Cardstock
Patterned scrapbook papers
Markers
Embossed papers
Decoupage medium
Stickers such as Ki Memories
Chipboard letters
Chipboard shapes
Buttons
Gel shapes
Glitter
Ribbon
Metal numbers such as Making
    Memories
Die-cut numbers such as Quikutz
Scrapbooking ink such as Tim Holtz
    Distressing Ink by Ranger
Magnetic tape

HERE'S HOW

For the cookie sheet background

1. Be sure cookie sheet is clean and dry.
Prime cookie sheet using spray primer.
2. Paint cookie sheet using acrylic paint.
3. Select 12×12-inch sheet of cardstock
for calendar grid. Trim cardstock width to
fit within edges of cookie sheet. Draw
calendar grid in pencil and then use
marker to go over grid.
4. Arrange patterned papers and calendar
as shown trimming as needed to fit cookie
sheet. Use decoupage medium to adhere
papers to cookie sheet. Let dry. Add 2 or
3 additional coats of decoupage medium
over entire cookie sheet to seal.
5. After decoupage medium is dry, glue
letters to top part of cookie sheet.

For the day-of-the-month pieces

The 25 pieces for the 25 days of
December are all different and are all
backed with a small piece of magnetic
tape so they cling to the cookie sheet.
Use pieces of chipboard as a base to
create many of the days. Add gel shapes,

glitter, additional small pieces of
chipboard, and buttons to the main
pieces of chipboard to create the
individual magnets. See photos on pages
38–39 for ideas. Also look for purchased
dice or game pieces, premade chipboard
shapes, small toys, and small cookie
cutters to use as day-of-the-month pieces.

Baby's First Christmas Album

Shown on pages 40, 41

WHAT YOU NEED

Chipboard
Die-cut machine and die-boards such
    as AccuCut
Trimmer
Scissors
Circle cutter
Patterned paper
Paper adhesive such as a glue stick
    or adhesive tape
Heavy-duty punch tool such as
    Crop-a-Dile
Acrylic paint
Ink-type chalk such as Colorbox Fluid
    Chalk
Dimensional stickers
Sticker letters, and tags such as K& Co.
Glitter glue such as Stickles
Ribbon
Metal rings
Buttons

HERE'S HOW

1. Using a die-cut machine and
die-boards, cut 5-6 scalloped shapes from
chipboard to create album cover and
pages. (The pages of the album shown
are made from scalloped squares.
Circle shapes are interspersed within
the album.)
2. Paint the edges of the chipboard with
acrylic paint and let dry.
3. Cut the same number of die-cut
shapes from coordinated patterned paper
and cardstock.
4. Using a glue stick or tape adhesive,
adhere cardstock and patterned paper
to either side of each chipboard page as
desired. (In the sample album, patterned
paper is on the left-hand page and
cardstock is the right.) Ink the edges
of each page as desired.

5. Mark the position of three holes along the left side of the album pages. Punch holes through the chipboard pages using the punch tool.

6. Hook pages together with metal rings.

7. Cut and ink cardstock photo mats for each right-hand album page. Adhere photos to the photo mats.

8. Incorporate a poem and journaling on the album pages.

9. Embellish the photos and pages as desired using glitter glue, dimensional stickers, buttons, and ribbon.

10. Use sticker letters and buttons to trim the front cover of the album.

11. Tie ribbon to the album rings.

BABY'S FIRST CHRISTMAS POEM

There's a beautiful tree
With many bright colors
For Baby to see
Along baby's crib
Bells that jingle are strung
And close by the chimney
Baby's stocking is hung.

On baby's first Christmas
There's wonderful joy
In giving to baby
That first special toy,
A ball or a rattle,
A soft teddy bear
That baby will cuddle
And take everywhere.

On baby's first Christmas
It's easy to find
That one tiny child
Brings another to mind
For baby reminds us
In a tangible way
That Jesus was born
On that first Christmas day.

— Jill Wolf

Mirrored Christmas Shapes
Shown on page 42

WHAT YOU NEED
Tracing paper
Pencil
Scissors
Small pre-cut round mirrors (available at crafts stores)
Fabric glue
Metallic and matching embroidery threads
Narrow cording, cut into 10-inch lengths
Small pieces polyester fiberfill

HERE'S HOW

1. Trace patterns, *page 50*, and cut out. Cut felt shapes from patterns. Cut holes from centers of felt to be placed over mirrors, cutting just slightly smaller than the mirror to be placed behind them. Make hand buttonhole stitches, *see page 160*, using 2 strands of embroidery floss around inside circle openings on felt. Glue mirrors in place on front background felt pieces. Place felt shape over mirrors and pin in place over front felt piece. Using 2 strands of embroidery floss, make hand buttonhole stitches around overlay felt.

2. Fold narrow cording in half to make a loop and tack in place at top inside of back felt piece. Place front over back felt and stitch together along outside edges, using 2 strands floss and buttonhole stitch. Leave opening along one side to lightly stuff with fiberfill batting. Hand-sew opening closed.

49

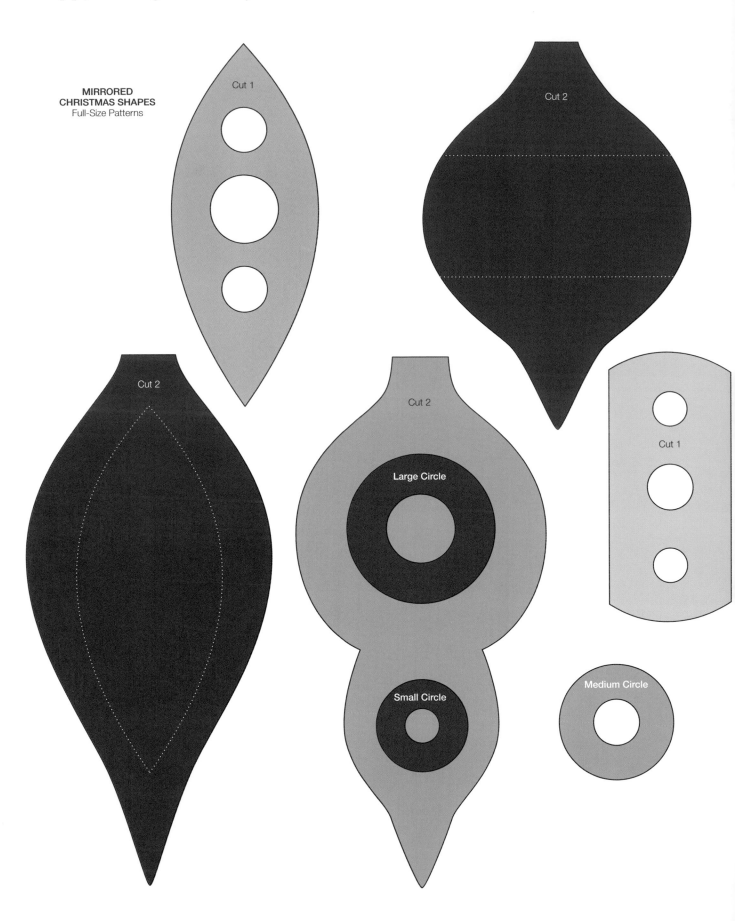

MIRRORED CHRISTMAS SHAPES
Full-Size Patterns

Cut 1

Cut 2

Cut 2

Cut 2

Cut 1

Large Circle

Small Circle

Medium Circle

MIRRORED
CHRISTMAS STOCKING
Enlarge 200%
Cut 2

Mirrored Christmas Stocking
Shown on page 43

WHAT YOU NEED
Tracing paper
Pencil; scissors
Two 9×14-inch pieces red glitter felt
Assorted small scraps multicolored felt
13 round pre-cut mirrors (available at
   crafts stores)
Fabric glue
Metallic or matching colors
   embroidery floss

HERE'S HOW
1. Enlarge and trace pattern, *above*, and cut out. Cut stocking back and front from red felt. Cut circles from contrasting-color scrap felt pieces for surrounding mirrors. Cut out centers of circles so openings are just slightly smaller than the mirror to be placed behind them. Position mirrors onto stocking front and glue in place.
2. Embroider buttonhole stitches, see *page 160*, using 2 strands of floss, around insides of each felt circle. Pin felt circles over mirrors on stocking front. Using 2 strands of floss, embroider buttonhole stitches around outside edges of circles.

3. Cut strip of felt ¾×8½ inches for hanging loop. Fold loop in half and tack with several hand stitches to side edge inside back piece of stocking.
4. With wrong sides together, place stocking front on top of stocking back and stitch together with blanket stitch. Stitch around top edges of front with blanket stitch, see *page 160*.

Winter

came down to our home one night
Quietly pirouetting in on
silvery-toed slippers of snow,
And we, we were children once again.

Bill Morgan, Jr

Snowflake Message Frame

Shown on page 44

WHAT YOU NEED

Frame and mat without glass
Computer
Cardstock
Felt shapes
Glitter glue
"Bling" dots such as Doodlebug
Flat glue dots
Dimensional foam dots
Scissors

HERE'S HOW

1. Select a frame and mat in an appropriate size. (Shown is an 8×10-inch frame with 5×7-inch mat.)
2. Select a winter or Christmas quote and type it on the computer. Resize the quote to fit the opening of the mat. Print and adjust as needed, then print the final copy on cardstock. Cut to fit inside frame.
3. Place the quote and mat inside the frame and attach the frame backing.
4. Embellish the mat and frame with felt shapes in coordinated colors by gluing

directly to the frame and mat. Shapes can be purchased or cut on a die-cut machine.
5. Decorate some of the felt shapes with glitter glue and self-adhesive "bling" dots. Adhere to the frame and mat using small, flat glue dots. Use dimensional dots under some of the shapes to provide dimension.

Bright Gift Card Tin

Shown on page 45

WHAT YOU NEED

Small top-open tin such as
    Provo Craft
Patterned paper
Glitter stickers
Clear tags
Ribbon
Ball chain (available at crafts stores)
Trimmer; scissors
1½-inch and ¼-inch hole punches
Strong crafts adhesive
Adhesive such as Tacky Tape
Decoupage medium such as
    Diamond Glaze
Dimensional foam dots

HERE'S HOW

1. Cut a strip of patterned paper to fit
around the middle of the tin. Adhere
with strong adhesive.
2. Cut and adhere a narrower strip
of coordinating paper to fit around the
lower portion of the tin.
3. Adhere a strip of ribbon around
the top edge of the paper.

4. Embellish the front of the tin with
glitter stickers. Use foam dots behind one
or more of the stickers to add dimension
and interest.
5. Hang a variety of punched tags and
embellishments from a short ball chain
attached to the tin's handle. In the
example, two clear tags are used, along
with a punched cardstock circle trimmed
with a snowflake sticker. (Cover the
punched circle with decoupage medium
to seal it and create the look of epoxy.)
6. Tie coordinating ribbon to the handle
of the tin.
7. Place gift card and a personal note
inside the tin.

Paper Gift Card Holders

Shown on page 45

WHAT YOU NEED

Double-sided patterned paper
Glitter stickers, and clear tags such
    as Making Memories
Ribbon
Trimmer
Scoring tool
Wavy trimmer such as Creative
    Memories
Scissors
1-inch, 1¼-inch and ¼-inch hole
    punches
Library pocket template
Circle cutter
Glitter glue
Gift card holder die-cut such as
    AccuCut

Die-cut letters, tab, and photo corners
    such as QuicKutz
Temporary adhesive tape
Tape adhesive such as Tacky Tape
Decoupage medium such as
    Diamond Glaze
Foam dimensional dots

HERE'S HOW FOR THE
FOLDING CARD

1. Cut a strip of double-sided patterned
paper measuring 3×10½ inches.
Measuring from the left-hand side, score
at 1½ inches. Measuring from the right-
hand side, score at 4¼ inches. Fold at
score lines.
2. Trim to round corners of gift card
holder and ink edges.
3. Make a pocket for the gift card using
a strip of patterned paper and strong
crafts adhesive.
4. Embellish the remainder of the gift
card holder as desired using stickers and
ribbon. In the sample a wavy trimmer was
used to create the pocket and trim on the
inside and front of the card.
5. To make a closure for the card as
shown on the front, adhere a decorated
cardstock punched circle just below the
top flap. Put tape adhesive only on the
lower portion of the punched circle.
Slip the flap under the punched circle.

HERE'S HOW FOR THE FLOWERED GIFT CARD

1. Using a template, cut a library pocket from double-sided patterned paper. Adhere using strong adhesive and ink edges.

2. Embellish front of pocket with coordinating patterned paper, ribbon, and glitter glue.

3. Back a clear decorative tag with a circle cut from cardstock. Decorate with glitter glue and ribbon. Adhere to the front of the pocket using dimensional foam dots.

4. Print a seasonal greeting on coordinating cardstock. Trim with a die-cut tab and matching paper, then insert into pocket along with gift card.

HERE'S HOW FOR THE ARGYLE GIFT CARD

1. Using a die-cut machine and die-board, cut a gift card holder from double-sided patterned paper. Fold on score lines and ink edges.

2. Prepare a "To/From" card and adhere to the outside of the gift card holder. Use stickers or die-cut letters, photo corners, and stickers to decorate the card.

3. Print a seasonal greeting, embellish with patterned paper and stickers, and adhere to the lower portion of the inside of the card. Insert gift card.

4. Make a closure for the card by adhering a glitter sticker to a punched cardstock sticker. Adhere the top of the punched circle to the flap of the gift card holder, then use a temporary adhesive under the lower portion of the punched circle. The recipient will be able to open the gift card holder easily.

Clever Christmas Organizer
Shown on pages 46–47

WHAT YOU NEED

Tin (available at scrapbooking stores)
Cardstock
Patterned paper
Stickers
Chipboard
Die-cut tabs and photo corners such
    as QuicKutz
Ribbon; glitter glue
Small hole punch
Trimmer; scissors
Adhesives such as Tacky Tape

HERE'S HOW FOR THE TIN

1. Cut 1-inch strips of patterned paper to fit around the bottom of the tin. Use a strong adhesive to adhere the paper.

2. Adhere a length of narrow ribbon around the top edge of the paper. Cut wider strips of paper to adhere to the front and back of the tin lid. Trim with narrow strips of cardstock.

3. Adhere patterned paper to the outside and inside of the bottom of the tin.

4. Embellish the tin as desired by adding holly leaves, glitter glue, and chipboard tags. Tie ribbon to the handle.

HERE'S HOW FOR THE DIVIDER CARDS

1. Determine the categories for the divider cards, such as a calendar, Christmas card list, decorating ideas, entertaining, gifts, receipts, recipes, secret Santa, and thank yous. Cut the divider cards from cardstock, making sure that the tin will fully close when full (cards shown measure 3½×4½ inches).

2. Print Christmas quotations (or use pre-printed quotes) to add to each card.

3. Decorate the front of each card as desired using coordinated patterned paper, stickers, and glitter glue.

4. Trim some divider cards with scalloped cardstock and ribbon.

5. Print or write labels for each card and attach to tabs.

6. Behind each divider card, place appropriate organizational tools such as a small calendar, a blank list for keeping track of Christmas cards, a gift idea list, etc. Customize as desired.

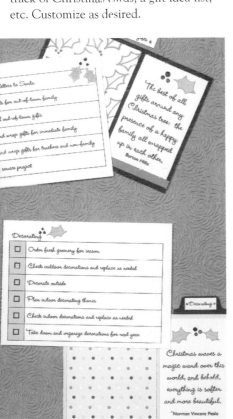

beautifully beribboned

Gather those lovely holiday ribbons and use them to decorate your home with yards of Christmas cheer.

Make a simple yet elegant statement by creating your own **Christmas Rose,** *above,* using wire-edge ribbon. Showcase the sweet rose in a clear rose bowl for a lovely holiday table favor. Wrap a pretty stocking in a taffeta ribbon when you make a beautiful **Holiday Bow Stocking,** *opposite.* The ribbons are sewn into the side seams and the bow is tied to form the cuff. For patterns and instructions, see pages 64–65.

Pretty satin ribbons are looped over and over to create an **Ever-Green Ribbon Tree,** *opposite below.* The structure is a plastic foam cone and the ribbons form the branches. A simple piece of ribbon becomes a playful **Ribbon Candy Ornament,** *opposite above,* to hang on your Christmas tree or in a window. Simple jingle bells and bright ribbon combine to make a **Jingle Bell Garland,** *above.* Instructions for all of the projects are on pages 65–66.

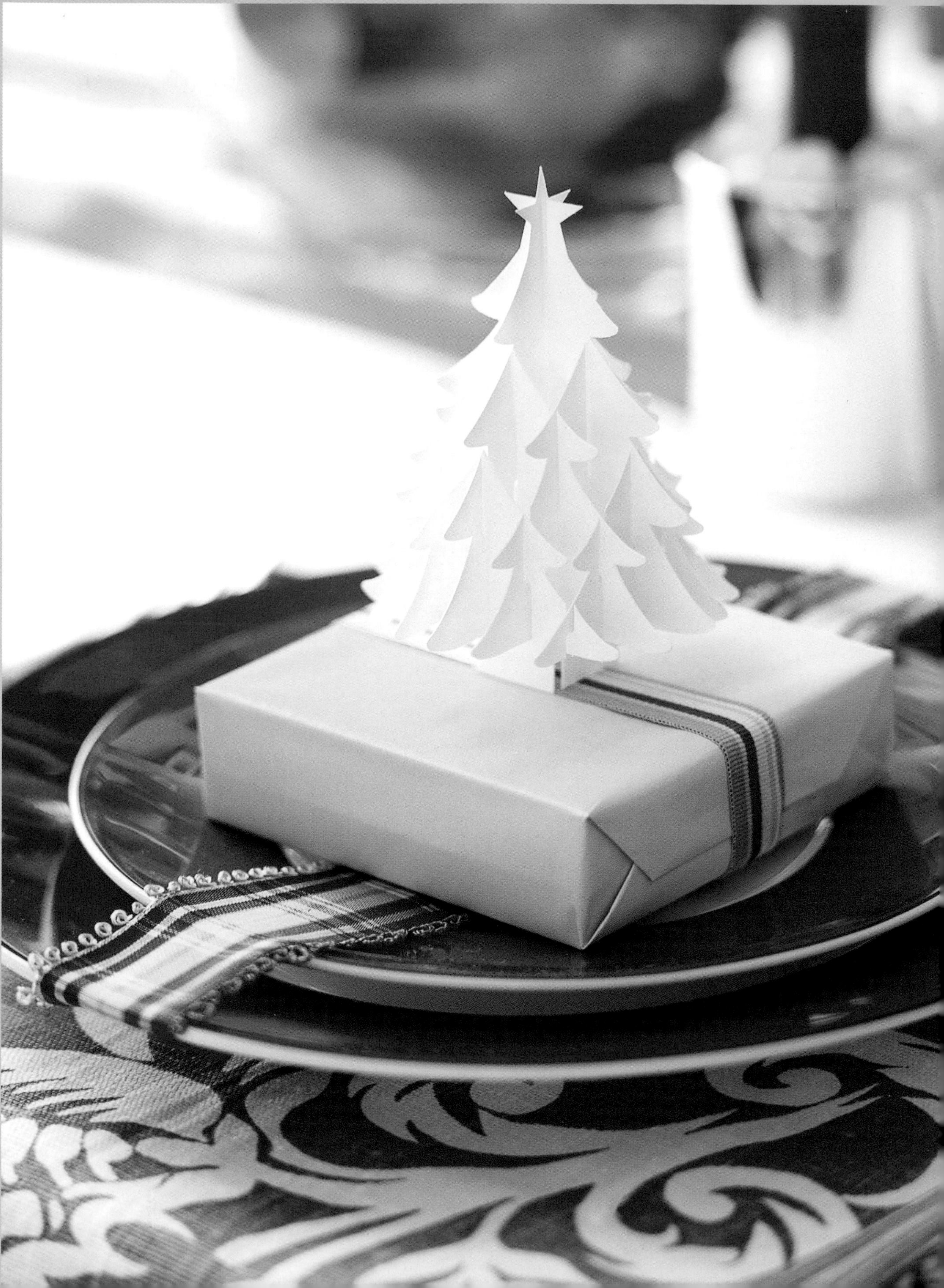

Create your own **Wrapped-Up Table Setting**, *opposite,* to set the mood for the season. A **Ribbons and Trims Room Divider**, *above,* is easy to customize by adjusting the length of the ribbons and ornaments. Use the divider between rooms or in a window. Add a **Photo Ribbon,** *right,* to your Christmas decorating or to a special gift. For instructions, see pages 67–68.

Striped ribbon is intertwined on this **Pretty Plaid Package**, *above left.*

Just add a candy cane and card to complete the look. Fill a jar with favorite

goodies and then decorate with ribbon to make a **Beribboned Jar**, *above*

right, that everyone will love. Decorate a section of your home with ribbons

to create a **Cupboard Ribbon Wrap**, *opposite.* Top off the cupboard with

tiny trees set in wrapped boxes. Instructions for all of the projects are on

pages 68–69.

back using ½-inch seam allowance. Clip curves, turn, and press.

5. Cut a strip of lime green fabric 2×8 inches for a hanging loop. Fold long edges right sides together and stitch using ¼-inch seam. Turn right side out and press. Fold loop in half and baste to top edge of stocking, raw edges even.

6. Place stocking inside lining pieces, right sides together. Stitch around top edge in ½-inch seam allowance, keeping an opening in the back to turn stocking right side out. Pull stocking through opening and work the lining back inside the stocking. Pin opening closed and hand sew together using matching thread. Press top edge so seam is flat.

7. Tie ribbons into a bow and trim ends.

Holiday Bow Stocking
Shown on page 56

WHAT YOU NEED
Tracing paper; pencil
Scissors
¾ yard lime green linen taffeta fabric
⅓ yard iron-on fleece
Two 32-inch lengths of 5-inch-wide heavy-weight ribbon
Matching sewing thread
1½ yards of ⅜-inch-wide cording

HERE'S HOW
1. Enlarge and trace stocking pattern, *right*. Cut 4 stocking pieces from taffeta; 2 for stocking and 2 for inside lining. Cut 2 stocking pieces from iron-on fleece. Trim ½ inch around all edges of fleece pieces and iron on back sides of green stocking pieces.

2. Cut bias strips 1¾ inches wide, joining together to make length of 54 inches. With right sides together, sew lining pieces together around side and lower edges, using a ½-inch seam allowance.

3. Gather ends of ribbon ⅜ inch from cut edges. Pull up threads to make ribbon ends 3½ inches wide. Place ribbon 1½ inches down from the top edge of stocking and baste gathered ribbon edge to side edge of stocking front.

4. Cover cording with strip of lime green fabric, basting close to cording. Baste covered cording to side and lower edges of stocking front. Sew stocking front to

Ribbon Placement

Ribbon Placement

HOLIDAY BOW STOCKING
Enlarge 250%
Cut 4, reversing two
from taffeta
Cut 2, reversing one
from iron-on fleece

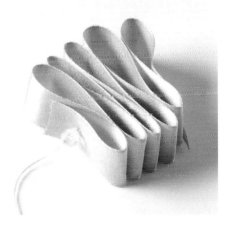

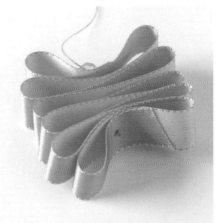

Christmas Rose
Shown on page 57

WHAT YOU NEED

1 yard 1½-inch-wide pink wire-edge
   ribbon
Masking tape
Scissors
Fine wire
Clear glass rose bowl

HERE'S HOW

1. Lay the ribbon on a flat surface. Locate
where the wire starts on one side of the
ribbon. On the other end of the ribbon,
bend the ribbon at the end and secure
with masking tape to keep the wire from
pulling out.

2. Starting with the exposed wire, gently
pull the wire slightly gathering the one
side of the wire. Remove the masking
tape and adjust that gathered side. Coil
the gathered ribbon around forming a
rose shape keeping the bottom tightly
closed. Secure with fine wire. Place the
ribbon rose in the glass rose bowl.

Ribbon Candy Ornament
Shown on page 58

WHAT YOU NEED

8-inch length of 1-inch wide satin
   ribbon in desired color and pattern
Paper clip
Needle; scissors
Thread to match ribbon colors
Small bead

HERE'S HOW

1. Gently fold the ribbon back and forth
accordion-style, making the loops about
1½ inches wide. Secure with a paper clip.

2. Thread the needle using two strands
of thread. Tie a knot at one end.

3. Remove the paper clip and, starting at
the bottom of the folds, place the needle
and thread through the center of the
folded ribbons. Pull the needle up
through the ribbons with the knot at
the bottom. Adjust the ribbon folds to
resemble ribbon candy. Make a tiny stitch
at the top of the ribbon folds to secure.

4. String bead onto thread and move to
top of ribbon. Cut the thread leaving
enough to hang the ribbon ornament.

Ever-Green Ribbon Tree

Shown on page 58

WHAT YOU NEED
Low-heat glue gun and glue sticks
2⅞×5⅞-inch foam cone such as
  Styrofoam
5½ yards lime green satin wire-edged
  ribbon, 2½ inches wide
2-inch glitter star ornament
Scissors

HERE'S HOW
Cut ribbon to lengths for each layer
of the tree:
7 6-inch pieces
7 5½-inch pieces
6 5-inch pieces
5 4½-inch pieces
4 4-inch pieces
4 3½-inch pieces
4 3-inch pieces
3 2½-inch pieces
1 4-inch piece for point
1 7-inch piece for top

1. Fold all but the last two lengths of
ribbon, wrong sides together with cut
edges even, keeping sizes separated.
2. Starting about an inch from the
bottom of the cone, gather cut edges of
longest lengths of ribbon slightly and glue
onto cone, distributing lengths around
foam shape. Glue next level about an
inch above first bottom layer, gathering
folded ribbon slightly as you glue it to
the cone. Continue gluing progressively
shorter lengths of ribbon in layers to
reach the top point of the cone.
3. For top point, fold 4-inch piece of
ribbon with long sides together, then fold
in half the opposite way to bring cut
edges together. Gather together bottom
cut edges and glue to top of foam cone.
4. To cover cut edges of top point and
the final layer of ribbon at the top, use
a 7-inch piece of ribbon. Fold under the
cut edge ¼ inch and glue to wrong side
of ribbon at both edges. Gather together
one end and glue to top of tree so that
horizontal length of ribbon goes around
top edge. Bunch up ribbon to form a
loop, pinch together to gather the
section, and glue in place over cut edges
of previous levels.
5. Continue making a couple of loops
around top edge of tree. Glue final folded
edge in place by gathering end and
joining it to the start of this ribbon length.
6. Cut a slit in the top fold of the tree
top point and glue star just inside the cut,
or glue bow ornament to tree front just
under top point.

Jingle Bell Garland

Shown on page 59

WHAT YOU NEED
Large jingle bells
Patterned ribbon
Sheer ribbon
Scissors

HERE'S HOW
Lay out jingle bells on a flat surface about
3 inches apart. Cut the sheer ribbon to a
length about 12 inches longer than the
line of bells. String the bells on the
ribbon. Cut small pieces of patterned
ribbon and tie between the bells.

Wrapped-Up Table Setting
Shown on page 60

WHAT YOU NEED
Wrapped package
Striped ribbon in two widths
Adhesive
Purchased 3-D paper tree or other
   paper trim
Plate and charger to match ribbon
Scissors

HERE'S HOW
Cut a small piece of the narrower width
ribbon and wrap around the package.
Secure with adhesive. Attach the tree
or other 3-D shape on top of the ribbon
with adhesive. Set aside. Place the plate
on the charger. Wrap the wider width
ribbon around the two pieces and tuck
under. Set the package on top of the plate.

Ribbons and Trims
Room Divider
Shown on page 61

WHAT YOU NEED
10 purchased apple-green Christmas
   ornaments
Narrow pink satin ribbon
1 yard striped 2-inch-wide pink ribbon
Yardstick
Scissors

HERE'S HOW
1. Lay the ornaments on a table in the
desired arrangement starting with 4 on
the bottom row, 3 on the next row, 2 on
the next, and 1 at the top. Adjust the
arrangement to fit the window or area
where the divider will hang.
2. Measure and cut the narrow ribbon
to connect to the ornaments allowing
5 more inches for tying.
3. Tie the ribbons between the
ornaments. Add a longer ribbon at the
top for hanging. Make a bow from the
striped ribbon and tie at the top.

Photo Ribbon
Shown on page 61
WHAT YOU NEED
Black and white photo
Cardstock; scissors
Striped scrapbook paper
Adhesive
Decorative brads
Red satin ribbon

HERE'S HOW

Measure the photo and cut the cardstock to accommodate the positioning of the photo. Cut a piece of striped scrapbook paper slightly larger than the cardstock. Adhere the photo to the cardstock and then to the scrapbook paper. Add two decorative brads at the top of the cardstock. Cut a length of ribbon slightly longer than the piece. Adhere piece to the ribbon and add a bow at the top.

Pretty Plaid Package

Shown on page 62

WHAT YOU NEED

Wrapped package
Scissors
Lengths of two different striped ribbons
Adhesive
Candy cane and card to match ribbon

HERE'S HOW

1. Cut two lengths of each of the striped ribbons long enough to wrap around the wrapped package both ways.
2. Using the same ribbon pattern, wrap one length each way securing it on the back of the package with adhesive. Tuck the other ribbon pattern under then over the long ribbons, securing it in the back.

3. Place the final ribbon piece over then under the first two ribbons forming a plaid design. Secure in the back. Tuck the candy cane and card under where the woven ribbons meet.

Beribboned Jar

Shown on page 62

WHAT YOU NEED

Purchased glass jar
Scrap of printed scrapbook paper
Pencil
Scissors
Striped ribbon in colors to match paper
Strong adhesive
Sheer white ribbon
Edible goodies
Ornament in color to match paper

HERE'S HOW

1. Be sure the jar is clean and dry.
2. Take the lid off the jar and trace around it to make a circle of paper using the scrapbook paper.
3. Cut out the circle.
4. Measure and cut a piece of ribbon long enough to fit around the center of the jar.
5. Center and overlap the ribbon at the back of the jar and glue to the jar. Glue the paper to the top of the jar lid. Let dry.

6. Fill the jar with desired goodies and put the lid on the jar.
7. Tie the sheer ribbon around the jar lid.
8. Cut another length of striped ribbon and fold it back and forth forming loops at both ends. Tie the ends of the sheer ribbon around the loops forming a bow.
9. Tie the ornament on the bow using the ends of the sheer ribbon.

Cupboard Ribbon Wrap

Shown on page 63

WHAT YOU NEED

Lengths of ribbon long enough to crisscross in the cupboard area
Yardstick
Scissors
Iron
Thumbtacks
Button or other embellishment
Strong crafts glue
Boxes
Printed wrapping paper with pink motif
1-inch-wide pink ribbon
Small artificial lighted trees

HERE'S HOW

1. Measure and cut the ribbon to fit inside the cupboard door. Iron the ribbons. Remove glass from doors. Crisscross the ribbons on the inside of the doors and secure in place using the thumbtacks. Replace glass. Adhere a pretty button or embellishment where the ribbons crisscross.

2. Wrap the boxes with the wrapping paper. Glue a ribbon around the middle of the boxes. Place a tree inside each box. Place the boxes on the cupboard.

All About Ribbon

All kinds of wonderful ribbons are available at crafts stores, fabric stores, scrapbook stores, and discount stores.

Ribbon can be purchased by the yard or by the roll. Buying on the roll is usually more economical. However, buying more expensive ribbons by the yard offers the opportunity to choose these ribbons if just a little of the beautiful ribbon is needed.

Ribbon is made from a variety of fibers including satin, silk, cotton, or even paper. The style of the ribbon or how it is woven also varies. There is grosgrain ribbon, satin-faced ribbon, sheer-woven ribbon, and printed ribbon.

Some ribbon has a wired edge which gives it more body to hold a shape. Other ribbon has no wire in the edge and flows naturally. Each style of ribbon offers lovely results.

Check out these websites featuring ribbon manufacturers, retail stores, and online stores. Look for new ribbon lines, check out favorites, and find retail outlets in your area.
www.craftopia.com
www.doodlebug.ws
www.hancockfabrics.com
www.joannfabrics.com
www.jordanpapercrafts.com
www.mjtrim.com
www.papermart.com
www.offray.com
www.michaels.com
www.midoriribbon.com
www.ribbonlady.com
www.ribbonshop.com

open house
nibbles & sips

Bring together a few festive drinks, some well-chosen appetizers, and a house full of your favorite people, and you have the makings of a fun holiday open house. The recipes in this chapter are all you need. Just set the date and invite your friends.

For a taste of tradition, pour glasses of **Apple Cider Punch**, *above*, a classic recipe from the 1930s. For an all-new sip, go for **Icy Cranberry Margaritas**, *opposite*. Either will taste delightful with **Cheddar-Pecan Crackers**, *opposite*. Recipes are on page 78.

Offer Tex-Mex flavors to put everyone in a spirited mood. **Mexican Fondue,** *opposite bottom,* combines cheese and chorizo to produce irresistible results. Hearty **Mini Mexican Tortas,** *opposite top,* provide bite-size versions of a classic south-of-the-border sandwich. For dessert, a twist on a Texan favorite, the **Chocolate-Malted Sheet Cake,** *above,* will complete your Tex-Mex theme. Recipes are on pages 78–79.

Spicy Cajun Shrimp, *above,* brings snappy seasonings to an always-popular seafood. How can you go wrong? Miniature phyllo dough shells make elegant **Tomato Quiche Tartlets,** *opposite top,* much easier than they look. Warm, oozy dips are always party favorites. **White Chili Dip,** *opposite below,* will prove a tasty example when served with crisp tortilla chips. Recipes are on page 80.

This year, serve updated takes on favorite party foods. Jalapeño pepper jelly imparts a sweet-hot edge to **Crunchy Munchies**, *below.* Hard-cooked eggs go global with **Greek-Style Deviled Eggs** and **Indian-Style Deviled Eggs**, *opposite,* both takes on the classic. Recipes are on page 81.

Icy Cranberry Margaritas

Shown on page 70

WHAT YOU NEED

½   cup frozen cranberry-raspberry juice concentrate, thawed
½   cup tequila
¼   cup orange liqueur
3   tablespoons melon liqueur
5   cups ice cubes
     Light-colored corn syrup (optional)
     Multicolored coarse decorating sugar (optional)

HERE'S HOW

1. In a blender combine juice concentrate, tequila, orange liqueur, and melon liqueur. Cover and blend until combined.
2. With blender running, add ice cubes one at a time through opening in lid, blending until slushy. If desired, dip rims of 6 glasses into corn syrup and then into decorating sugar placed in a shallow dish. Pour blended mixture into glasses. Makes 6 servings.

Cheddar-Pecan Crackers

Shown on page 70

WHAT YOU NEED

1   cup shredded cheddar cheese (4 ounces)
¼   cup butter
¼   teaspoon dried thyme, crushed
⅛   teaspoon cayenne pepper
¾   cup all-purpose flour
½   cup finely chopped pecans
2   tablespoons finely chopped pecans
     Nonstick cooking spray

HERE'S HOW

1. Place cheddar cheese and butter in a medium mixing bowl. Let stand at room temperature for 30 minutes.
2. Beat cheese mixture with an electric mixer on low to medium speed until combined. Add thyme and cayenne pepper. Beat until combined.
3. Using a wooden spoon, stir in flour and the ½ cup finely chopped pecans. Form into a ball. Shape into an 8-inch-long log. Roll log in the 2 tablespoons pecans. Wrap log in plastic wrap. Chill about 4 hours or until the mixture is firm.
4. Preheat oven to 350°F. Lightly coat baking sheets with nonstick cooking spray. Using a sharp knife, cut log into ⅛-inch slices. Bake about 10 minutes or until light brown. Transfer to wire racks and let cool. Makes about 60 crackers.
To store: Store in a tightly covered container in refrigerator for up to 1 week.

Apple Cider Punch

Shown on page 71

WHAT YOU NEED

6   cups apple cider
2   cups cranberry-raspberry juice, orange juice, or orange-mango juice
½   cup lemon juice
1   750-ml bottle sparkling white grape juice or sparkling wine

HERE'S HOW

1. In a punch bowl or large pitcher combine apple cider, cranberry-raspberry juice, and lemon juice. Slowly add sparkling white grape juice. Serve immediately. Makes 11½ cups (about fifteen 6-ounce servings).

Mini Mexican Tortas

Shown on page 72. Choose sweet or spicy peppers according to your taste. Pepperoncini salad peppers are a good choice.

WHAT YOU NEED

1   17-ounce package refrigerated cooked pork roast au jus
¼   cup chopped purchased pickled chile peppers or ⅓ cup chunky salsa
¼   cup snipped fresh cilantro
2   tablespoons finely chopped red onion
2   tablespoons lime juice
2   cloves garlic, minced
¼   teaspoon salt
2   ripe avocados, seeded and peeled
8   tea- or cocktail-size buns (about 1½-inch diameter), split

HERE'S HOW

1. Place pork roast with juices in a medium saucepan. Using two forks, gently pull pork apart to shred. Stir in peppers and cilantro until combined. Cover pan and heat through over medium-low heat, stirring occasionally.
2. Meanwhile, in a medium bowl stir together onion, lime juice, garlic, and salt. Add avocados and coarsely mash until combined.
3. Use a slotted spoon or fork to transfer the pork mixture evenly onto bottom halves of the small buns. Top with avocado mixture and top halves of buns. Makes 8 mini-sandwiches.

cheese mixture to a fondue pot and keep warm. Serve with desired dippers. Makes about 3 cups (twelve ¼-cup servings).
*Note: Use additional Monterey Jack or whole-milk mozzarella if suitable Mexican cheese is not available.
**Test Kitchen Tip: To toast bread cubes, place French bread cubes on a baking sheet. Bake in a 350°F oven for 5 to 7 minutes or until crisp and toasted.

Mexican Fondue
Shown on page 72

WHAT YOU NEED

- 4 ounces uncooked chorizo sausage, casing removed
- ½ cup finely chopped yellow onion
- 1 to 3 teaspoons minced canned chipotle peppers in adobo sauce
- 1 clove garlic, minced
- 1 cup lager beer or chicken broth
- 8 ounces Monterey Jack cheese, shredded
- 8 ounces Mexican melting cheese, such as queso asadero or Chihuahua,* shredded or crumbled
- 1 tablespoon cornstarch
  Dippers, such as tortilla chips, cooked chicken chunks, toasted French bread cubes,** and assorted vegetable chunks (sweet peppers, zucchini, yellow squash, broccoli, and/or cherry tomatoes)

HERE'S HOW

1. In a medium saucepan cook chorizo over medium heat until browned. Drain all but 1 tablespoon fat. Add onion and cook for 5 to 7 minutes or until tender. Stir in chipotle peppers and garlic. Add beer; bring to a simmer.
2. In a large resealable plastic bag, combine cheeses and cornstarch. Seal bag; shake to coat cheeses with cornstarch. Add cheeses, a handful at a time, to saucepan, stirring until each addition is melted before adding more. Transfer

Chocolate-Malted Sheet Cake
Shown on page 73

WHAT YOU NEED

- 2 cups all-purpose flour
- 2 cups sugar
- ⅓ cup vanilla or chocolate malted milk powder
- 1 teaspoon baking soda
- ¼ teaspoon salt
- 1 cup butter
- 1 cup water
- ⅓ cup unsweetened cocoa powder
- 2 eggs
- ½ cup buttermilk or sour milk*
- 1½ teaspoons vanilla
- 2 cups malted milk balls, chopped
  Chocolate Buttermilk Frosting
  Red and green miniature candy-coated chocolate pieces

HERE'S HOW

1. Preheat oven to 350°F. Grease a 15×10×1-inch baking pan; set aside. In a very large bowl combine flour, sugar, malted milk powder, baking soda, and salt; set aside.
2. In a medium saucepan combine butter, water, and cocoa powder. Bring mixture just to boiling, stirring constantly. Remove from heat. Add the cocoa mixture to flour mixture and whisk or stir vigorously until thoroughly combined. Add eggs, buttermilk, and vanilla. Whisk or stir until combined (batter will be thin). Pour batter into the prepared pan.
3. Bake about 25 minutes or until a wooden toothpick inserted in the center comes out clean. Place cake in pan on a wire rack.
4. Sprinkle malted milk balls evenly over warm cake. Drizzle warm Chocolate-Buttermilk Frosting over the malted milk

balls. Cool thoroughly before cutting. If desired, sprinkle a few candy-coated chocolate pieces over the top. Serve cake the same day. Cover and store any remaining cake in the refrigerator for up to 24 hours. Makes 24 servings.
Chocolate-Buttermilk Frosting: In a medium saucepan combine ¼ cup butter or margarine, 3 tablespoons unsweetened cocoa powder, and 3 tablespoons buttermilk or milk. Bring to boiling. Remove from heat. Add 2¼ cups sifted powdered sugar and ½ teaspoon vanilla. Beat until smooth. Let frosting cool for 15 minutes or until slightly thickened, stirring occasionally, before drizzling over cake. If frosting sets up, add milk, 1 teaspoon at a time, until drizzling consistency is reached.
*Note: To make sour milk, place 1½ teaspoons lemon juice or vinegar in a 1-cup glass measuring cup. Add milk to make ½ cup. Stir and let stand 5 minutes.

Spicy Cajun Shrimp

Shown on page 74

WHAT YOU NEED

- 1 pound fresh or frozen large shrimp in shells
- ½ cup mayonnaise or salad dressing
- 2 tablespoons tomato paste
- 1 tablespoon lemon juice
- ½ teaspoon bottled minced garlic (1 clove)
- 2 tablespoons butter or margarine, melted
- 4 teaspoons Cajun seasoning

HERE'S HOW

1. Thaw shrimp, if frozen. Peel and devein shrimp, leaving tails intact. Rinse shrimp; pat dry with paper towels. In a small bowl stir together mayonnaise, tomato paste, lemon juice, and garlic. Cover and chill until ready to serve.

2. Brush both sides of each shrimp with melted butter. Sprinkle both sides of each shrimp with Cajun seasoning. Place on the unheated rack of a broiler pan.

3. Broil 4 to 5 inches from the heat for 2 minutes. Turn shrimp; broil for 1 to 2 minutes more or until shrimp are opaque. Serve shrimp with mayonnaise mixture. Makes 8 appetizer servings.

Tomato Quiche Tartlets

Shown on page 75

WHAT YOU NEED

- 2 2.1-ounce packages baked miniature phyllo dough shells (30 shells)
- ½ cup finely snipped dried tomatoes (not oil packed)
- 2 eggs, lightly beaten
- 3 tablespoons half-and-half, light cream, or milk
- 1½ teaspoons snipped fresh basil or ½ teaspoon dried basil, crushed Dash salt and ground black pepper
- ¾ cup finely shredded Swiss cheese

HERE'S HOW

1. Preheat oven to 325°F. Place phyllo dough shells on a baking sheet; set aside.

2. For filling, in a bowl combine tomato and enough boiling water to cover; let stand for 2 minutes. Drain well. In a bowl combine eggs, half-and-half, basil, salt, and pepper. Stir in tomato and cheese.

3. Spoon about 2 teaspoons of the filling into each phyllo shell. Bake for 10 to 15 minutes or until filling is slightly puffed and a small knife inserted into the centers of the tartlets comes out clean. Serve warm or cool. Makes 30 tartlets.

Make-Ahead Directions: Bake tartlets as directed; cool. Place tartlets in an airtight container. Cover; chill for up to 24 hours. Before serving, place tartlets on a baking sheet. Bake in a 300°F oven about 10 minutes or until heated through.

White Chili Dip

Shown on page 75

WHAT YOU NEED

- 1 15-ounce can great Northern beans, rinsed and drained
- ¾ cup bottled salsa
- 2 cups shredded Monterey Jack cheese with jalapeño peppers (8 ounces)
- ¼ cup milk
- 1 teaspoon ground cumin
- 2 cups chopped or shredded cooked chicken breast (12 ounces)
- ⅓ cup chopped pitted ripe olives (optional)
  Chopped tomato and chopped fresh jalapeño chile pepper*
  Tortilla chips

HERE'S HOW

1. In large saucepan combine beans, salsa, cheese, milk, and cumin. Cook over medium-low heat, stirring constantly, until cheese is melted.

2. Add cooked chicken and, if desired, the olives; heat through, stirring occasionally. Garnish with chopped tomato and jalapeño pepper. Serve with tortilla chips. Makes about 3½ cups.

***Note:** Because hot chile peppers, such as jalapeños, contain volatile oils that can burn your skin and eyes, avoid direct contact with chiles as much as possible. When working with chile peppers, wear plastic or rubber gloves. If your bare hands do touch the chile peppers, wash your hands well with soap and water.

Crunchy Munchies

Shown on page 76

WHAT YOU NEED

¼ cup jalapeño pepper jelly
2 tablespoons butter
¼ teaspoon five-spice powder
¼ teaspoon salt
¼ teaspoon bottled hot pepper sauce
2 cups whole cashews or
   dry roasted peanuts
1 cup dried banana chips
1 cup dried pineapple chunks,
   cut up
1 cup chopped pitted dates
1 cup chow mein noodles

HERE'S HOW

1. Preheat oven to 325°F. In a medium saucepan combine jelly, butter, five-spice powder, salt, and hot pepper sauce. Heat over low heat until jelly is melted. Stir in nuts, banana chips, pineapple, dates, and chow mein noodles until well coated. Pour mixture into a large roasting pan.

2. Bake for 15 to 20 minutes or until cashews are lightly browned, stirring once. Remove from oven. Spread mixture on a large piece of foil to cool. Makes about 6 cups.

To store: Place mixture in an airtight container. Cover and store at room temperature for up to 3 days.

Greek-Style Deviled Eggs

Shown on page 77

WHAT YOU NEED

7 hard-cooked eggs*
¼ cup mayonnaise or salad dressing
2 tablespoons feta cheese
1 tablespoon finely chopped pitted
   kalamata olives or other pitted
   ripe olives
2 teaspoons snipped fresh oregano
1 to 2 teaspoons Dijon-style
   mustard, balsamic herb mustard,
   honey mustard, or other favorite
   mustard
½ teaspoon dry mustard
   Salt
   Ground black pepper
   Several small fresh oregano leaves,
   fresh Italian (flat-leaf) parsley
   sprigs, or paprika (optional)

HERE'S HOW

1. Cut 6 of the eggs in half lengthwise or crosswise; gently remove the yolks and set the whites aside. Cut a small slice off bottoms of the egg white halves to help them stand up. Coarsely chop the remaining whole egg.

2. In a medium bowl combine egg yolks, chopped egg, mayonnaise, feta cheese, olives, oregano, Dijon-style mustard, and dry mustard. Season to taste with salt and black pepper.

3. Spoon egg yolk mixture into egg white halves. If desired, top with a small fresh oregano leaf, small sprig of fresh parsley, or paprika. Makes 12 halves.

Indian-Style Deviled Eggs: Prepare as directed, except omit mayonnaise, feta cheese, olives, oregano, and mustards. Fold 3 tablespoons plain low-fat yogurt, 1 tablespoon chopped chutney, and ½ teaspoon curry powder into yolk mixture. Omit herb or paprika garnish and top with chopped peanuts and chopped green onion.

***Note:** To hard-cook eggs, place eggs in a single layer in a large saucepan (do not stack eggs). Add enough cold water to cover the eggs by at least 1 inch. Bring to a rapid boil over high heat (water will have large, rapidly breaking bubbles). Remove from heat. Cover and let stand for 15 minutes; drain. Run cold water over the eggs or place them in ice water until cool enough to handle; drain. Peel off the egg shells. (For extra-large eggs, let them stand in the boiled water for 18 minutes.)

Make-Ahead Directions: Prepare filled eggs and place in an airtight container. Cover and chill in the refrigerator for up to 12 hours.

keepsake
ornaments

You will look forward to getting ornaments out of the box and onto the tree when the trims are handmade and from the heart.

Hear the sounds of the season when you create **Jingle Bell Trims,** *above,* to hang on the tree or on a pretty wreath. Create a **Wreath of Ornaments,** *opposite*, by starting with a purchased fresh evergreen wreath and adding handmade ornaments and a festive bow. Instructions for the projects are on page 94.

Even Santa would approve of **Santa's Tummy Trim,** *opposite,* made using a purchased red ornament and a touch of paint and glitter. Scrapbook paper printed on both sides twists into a **Pretty Paper Pinwheel,** *above.* Use these clever trims as ornaments or package toppers. Instructions and patterns are on pages 94–95.

Truly keepsake ornaments, beautiful **Christmas Lace Eggs,** *right and opposite,* are created using real eggs and a fine drill. The tiny designs, so intricately cut, make each lace egg a work of art. Instructions are on pages 95–96.

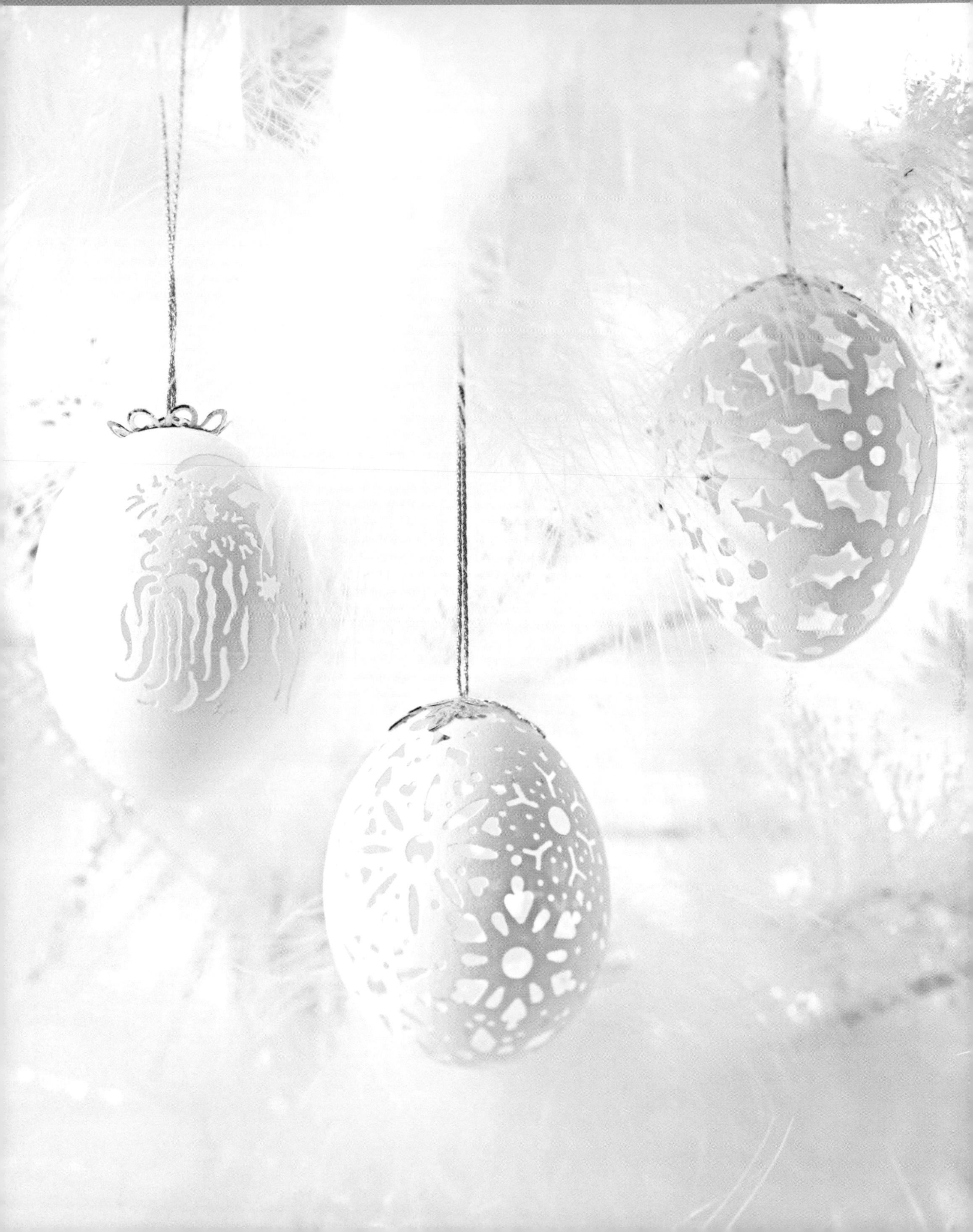

Find new fascination in those wonderful nail polish colors to make **Simple Swirls,** *opposite above.* With just a little paint and glitter, nature's pinecones become **Glittered Pinecones,** *opposite below,* in any color that fits your decorating scheme. Small purchased wooden stars are wrapped in wire and beads to become **Bedazzling Beaded Stars,** *below.* Instructions for the projects are on pages 96–97.

Hot glue melts almost like magic into **Icy Snowflakes,** *opposite above.*

Paint them or leave them transparent for a winter look. Let the

kids help make an easy **Origami Garland,** *opposite below,* that can

add sparkle to a mantel or tree. Textured yarns are wrapped to become

Balls of String Ornaments, *above,* that hold a much-appreciated

money gift. Instructions for all of the projects are on pages 97–99.

Fabric wraps round and round to make **Lollipop Ornaments,** *above,*
that are colorful and fun to make with fabric scraps. Bits of tapestry-like
fabric and fun fur combine to make stunning **Old World Santas,** *opposite*.
Tiny jingle bells adorn the Santa hats. Instructions and patterns for all
of the projects are on pages 99–101.

Wreath of Ornaments

Shown on cover and page 82

WHAT YOU NEED

16-inch fresh evergreen wreath
Jingle Bell Trims
Pretty Paper Pinwheels
Santa's Tummy Trim
Fine wire
Wire snips
Purchased candy lollipops (see
   Sources, page 160)
Wired red jewels (available at floral
   and crafts stores)
⅜-inch red patterned ribbon
2-inch-wide red patterned ribbon
Scissors

HERE'S HOW

Secure the ornaments on the wreath
using fine wire. Wire on the lollipops.
Poke the wired red jewels into the wreath
and secure with more fine wire. Wrap
the ⅜-inch patterned ribbon around the
wreath. Secure in the back of the wreath
by tying to the greenery. Make a bow
using the wide patterned ribbon. Wire
the bow to the top of the wreath.

Jingle Bell Trims

Shown on cover and pages 82–83

WHAT YOU NEED

Clear glass ornament with flat front
   (available at crafts stores)
About 20 small red jingle bells
8-inch-long piece of ⅜-inch-wide red
   patterned ribbon
Glass adhesive
Small felt tree shape (available at
   scrapbook stores)
¼-inch-wide apple green ribbon

HERE'S HOW

Take off the ornament top and add the
red jingle bells. Put the top back on the
ornament. Wrap the patterned ribbon
around the ornament and glue in place.
Glue felt tree shape where the ribbon
ends cross. Tie the apple green ribbon
in a bow at the top of the ornament.

Santa's Tummy Trim

Shown on cover and pages 82, 84

WHAT YOU NEED

Purchased red round ornament with
   pointed bottom
½-inch-wide double-stick tape
Black glitter
Glass paint in metallic gold
Fine tip brush

HERE'S HOW

Be sure the ornament is clean and dry.
Place the double-stick tape around the
middle of the ornament. Peel off one side
of the tape and dust with glitter. Shake
off any excess glitter. Carefully paint the
shape of a buckle over the glitter using
the glass paint. Let the paint dry.

Pretty Paper Pinwheel

Shown on cover and pages 82, 85

WHAT YOU NEED

Tracing paper
Scissors
Pencil
Ruler
7×7-inch square of scrapbook paper
   printed on both sides
Corsage pin or sharp point to poke hole
Small brad
Small paper punch
Fine ribbon

HERE'S HOW

1. Trace the pattern, *below*, and cut out, marking all lines on the pattern. Place the pattern on top of the square of scrapbook paper and cut along the lines as indicated on the pattern. Make a tiny hole at each dot using the corsage pin or sharp point.

2. Bring every other point of the paper to the center point overlapping the corners of the paper over the center dot. Put the small brad through the hole and open at the back to secure. Punch a hole in the top corner of the pinwheel and thread fine ribbon through the hole to hang. Or if using as a package trim, adhere to top of package using double-stick tape.

Christmas Lace Eggs

Shown on pages 86–87
For information see Sources, page 160

WHAT YOU NEED
Chicken eggs
Bulb syringe
Dishpan
Toothpicks
Bleach; 2 small bowls
Sponge/cloth
Egg carton

Matte acrylic spray
Rotary tool such as Dremel with cable
Assorted rotary tool drill bits
Jewelry findings
Metallic cord
Crafts glue
Scissors; pencil

HERE'S HOW

To prepare the egg

1. Drill ⅛-inch hole in each egg to be carved. This hole is often placed at the oblique round end of the egg opposite the more pointed end. *Note:* If you know where the design will be placed on the egg, the hole can be positioned to be integrated into the design.

2. Gently insert a toothpick through the hole to pierce the yolk.

3. Over the sink or a dishpan, place the tip of the bulb syringe gently but snuggly over the hole. Squeeze the syringe forcing air into the egg. After each squeeze allow time for the egg to dispense of its contents. *Note:* Emptying all the contents may require a couple of tries.

4. Continue pushing air in and allowing contents to drain until egg is empty.

5. Once the egg is empty, mix equal parts of bleach and water in one of the small bowls. Put plain water in the other bowl.

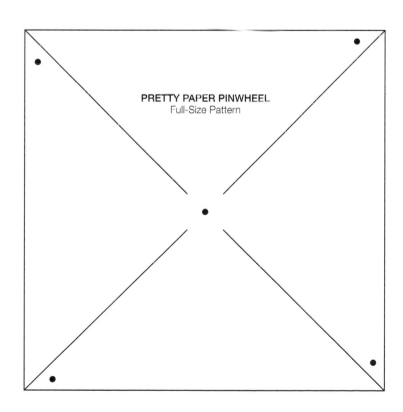

PRETTY PAPER PINWHEEL
Full-Size Pattern

6. Draw up the water/bleach solution into the syringe and inject it into the empty shell.

7. Cover the hole in the shell with your finger and shake gently.

8. Use syringe to remove the bleach solution over dishpan as you did the egg white and yolk.

9. Repeat six times with water to rinse.

10. Set eggshell in carton hole with the end down.

To put the design on the egg

1. The designs you choose must be stencil-like so pieces will not fall out.

2. Draw desired design on egg with pencil. Use very small stencils to put a design on the egg if drawing is difficult. Start with something simple with larger connecting pieces.

Note: Areas to be cut out can be shaded in with a pencil to make the design easier to carve.

3. Hold the egg in the palm of your hand rather than applying pressure with your fingertips. Using a fine drill bit in the rotary tool, gently make a pilot hole in a design area to be cut out. Then gently move the tool along the inside edge of line moving only as fast as the tool cuts. Do not force. Move the direction of the rotation of the tool.

4. Make small holes by simply piercing the egg, larger holes by circling the pilot hole, and lines moving in the direction the design indicates.

5. Make all cuts to complete the design.

6. When all areas are cut out, place the shell in a solution of 1 part bleach and 5 parts water in a small bowl to remove membrane on the inside of shell and pencil lines.

7. Once clean, rinse with water and set aside to dry.

8. When dry, carefully spray with matte acrylic spray and allow to dry.

9. Add jewelry finding and metallic cord.

Simple Swirls
Shown on page 88

WHAT YOU NEED
Purchased matte ornament
Old towel
Nail polish in desired color

HERE'S HOW
Lay the ornament on the towel. Using the nail polish brush that is in the polish, make simple designs such as swirls on one side of the ornament. Allow to dry. Turn the ornament over and repeat as for the first side. Allow to dry.

Glittered Pinecones
Shown on page 88

WHAT YOU NEED
Pinecones
Acrylic paint in desired colors
Paintbrush
Glitter to match paint colors
Top from purchased ornament
Strong crafts glue
Ribbon

HERE'S HOW
Be sure pinecone is clean and dry. Paint the pinecone using desired color of paint. While the paint is still wet, dust with glitter that matches the paint color. Allow the paint and glitter to dry. Glue the top from a purchased ornament to the top of the pine cone using a strong crafts glue. Allow to dry. Thread ribbon through top of ornament hook.

Bedazzling Beaded Stars

Shown on page 89

WHAT YOU NEED

Metallic fabric scraps in desired color
Fabric marker
Purchased wood star shapes
Fabric adhesive
Wire ornament hangers
Wire cutters
24-gauge gold wire
Small multicolored glass beads

HERE'S HOW

1. On back side of fabric, trace around wooden star two times, using the fabric marker. Cut one piece of fabric right on the lines and the other one about ⅜ inch outside of the marked lines. On the larger piece of fabric, clip in at inner points and clip fabric across outer points.
2. With wrong side of fabric up, place wooden star in center of fabric. Glue around outside edges of wooden star and pull excess fabric to the back of the wooden star. Place more glue over these fabric edges and place the wrong side of the smaller fabric piece over the back side of the wooden star to enclose the raw edges. Slide an ornament hanger between layers of fabric on the backside and press into glue.
3. Pull a length of wire from the spool and thread an assortment of glass beads onto the wire, keeping the length attached to the spool. With the cut wire edge, poke the end between fabric layers on the back to begin. Loop the wire over the front of the ornament shape, sliding

beads to the front as the wire is wrapped over and around, as desired. Clip the wire using wire cutters. Poke the end underneath other overlapping lengths of wire or between fabric layers at the side to secure the end.

Icy Snowflakes

Shown on page 90

WHAT YOU NEED

Tracing paper; pencil; scissors
Hot glue gun and glue sticks
Gold or silver spray paint
Freezer paper
Black fine-line marker
Masking tape
Water-filled container
Dishwashing liquid
Metallic thread

HERE'S HOW

1. Trace pattern, *page 98*, and cut out. Place patterns on work surface. Place plastic-coated side of freezer paper face down on top of patterns. Trace patterns onto freezer paper with black marker.

2. Tape traced patterns onto covered work surface with plastic-coated side facing up, leaving space between patterns.
3. With finger, spread a thin coat of dishwashing liquid over each traced pattern (*see Photo A, page 98*).
4. With glue gun, outline each pattern on the solid black lines (*see Photo B, page 98*). Allow glue to set firmly. Carefully peel ornaments from freezer paper. To remove soap residue, gently wash and dry the ornaments.
5. Lay dried ornaments on a covered surface. Spray front of each ornament with gold or silver paint. Do not spray back (flat) side. Let paint dry thoroughly before proceeding.
6. With the back (flat side) of one ornament facing upward, float ornament in water-filled container.
7. UNPLUG GLUE GUN before proceeding. While still hot, use glue gun to fill in outer points of shape, making sure glue comes in contact with the ornament outline (*see Photo C, page 98*). To give the look of crystal, do not completely fill in each outline.

97

keepsake ornaments

A

B

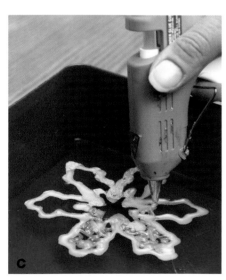

C

8. Carefully remove the ornament from water and pat dry.

9. For each ornament hanger cut an 8-inch length of metallic thread. Insert one length through top center of each ornament; tie ends together in an overhand knot.

Origami Garland
Shown on page 90

WHAT YOU NEED
Strips of decorative paper (heavy wrapping paper works well)
White glue; iridescent glitter
Fine gold metallic thread and needle
Puchased garland

HERE'S HOW
1. Cut paper into 12×½-inch strips for medium-sized stars. Start making the star by loosely tying the strip into a knot close to one end.

2. Pull on both ends of the strip so the edges of the strip come together to form a pentagon shape. Flatten the shape. The shape will have a long tail and a short tail.

3. Fold the shorter end against the pentagon and tuck it into the "pocket" created from folding. Turn the pentagon around and fold the longer end along the pentagon so the edges meet. Maintain the pentagon shape. Turn and fold again, making sure to fold along the edge to retain the shape of the pentagon.

4. Continue folding, making sure the folds are not too sharp, until most of the strip is folded and there is a short end remaining. Fold the short end against the pentagon and tuck it into the "pocket" (if the tail is too long, just fold over a bit of the end to make a shorter tail that fits neatly and securely into the pocket).

5. Hold the flat star between the forefinger and thumb of one hand. With a thumbnail from the other hand, gently make a dent into one side of the pentagon to begin to puff out the star. Rotate the star so that it puffs out on all five sides. If any edges stick out, apply a small amount of glue to seal in place.

6. Swirl thin lines of glue around the sides of the stars and sprinkle with iridescent glitter. Allow glue to dry.

7. Thread metallic thread through a small needle and poke through both sides of one star point. Knot ends of thread for an ornament or tie onto purchased garland for an added decoration.

ICY SNOWFLAKE
Full-Size Pattern

98

around and a small opening at the top balloon tie so the shape stays round. Using different colors and textures of cording provides extra interest. Lay ball on waxed paper to dry, rotating every few hours to allow all sides to dry. When completely dry, pop balloon and remove from top opening. Apply thin line of glue to some cordings and lightly shake glitter over outlined areas. Shake off excess and allow to dry again on waxed paper. Thread cording through top open areas across opening and knot ends to make hanging loop.

Lollipop Ornaments
Shown on page 92

WHAT YOU NEED
½-inch cording cut in lengths of
    23-27 inches
Striped fabric cut into strips
    1½-inch-wide×23-27 inches long
6-inch lollipop sticks
Matching thread; fabric glue
Thin cording cut in 9-inch lengths for
    hanging loop

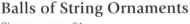

Dip cording in glue to coat. Squeeze out excess glue and wrap around balloon in crisscross or squiggly designs. Wrap balloon, leaving some openings all

Balls of String Ornaments
Shown on page 91

WHAT YOU NEED
Small water balloons
White glue; water
Small bowl
Desired colors of narrow cording or
    yarn, cut to 10-inch lengths
Iridescent glitter
Waxed paper

HERE'S HOW
1. Blow up balloons to make small round shapes and tie ends. In a small bowl make a solution of 2 parts glue and 1 part water.

keepsake ornaments

1. With right sides together, fold fabric in half lengthwise. Stitch long edge in ¼-inch seam. Turn right side out. Insert cording inside fabric tube. Fold raw edges of ends to inside and stitch closed using matching thread and small hand whip stitches. Curl fabric tube in a tight circle, using long pins to hold in place. On back side stitch rows together with hand stitches. Place lollipop stick in center back of coils, extending stick almost to the top. Stitch around stick and through back of coils to hold in place. Place fabric glue under top end of stick. Thread narrow cording under top row of coil, fold in half and knot ends to form hanging loop.

Old World Santas
Shown on page 93

WHAT YOU NEED
Tracing paper
Pencil
Scissors
Red satin fabric scraps
Cotton batting scraps
Fun fur scraps
Polyester fiberfill
Scrap flesh-colored cotton fabric
Double needle for sewing machine
   (40/80)
Flesh-color sewing thread
Rouge make-up and small brush
Black permanent fabric marker
Hot gun and glue sticks
6 mm red jingle bells
9 mm gold/silver jingle bells
Artificial holly leaves or greencry trim
Thin metallic thread and needle

HERE'S HOW
1. Trace full-size patterns, *opposite*, onto tracing paper. Cut out. Cut two Santa body patterns from red fabric. Cut one face pattern from flesh colored fabric. From cotton batting, cut one piece from beard pattern and one from face pattern. Cut one 1×7-inch piece of fun fur.
2. With right sides together, stitch around body pieces, using a ¼-inch seam allowance. Leave an opening at the bottom for stuffing. Turn and insert fiberfill through opening and stuff well. Stitch bottom edge together, using small hand whip-stitch and matching thread.
3. To make face, place flesh-colored fabric on top of batting layer. Glue face piece onto front of body.
4. Roll 1½×3-inch piece of batting, bringing long edges together. Glue in place around top curve of face for eyebrows. For beard, fold top edge of batting to back and glue in place. Glue top edge of beard to bottom of face piece. Glue remaining edges of beard in place, folding under the cut edges all around side and bottom. Bring long edges of fun fur together to make a roll. Glue edges together on the back of the fur. Glue fur around top edge of batting around face, bringing edges together at the back.
5. With permanent marker, make small dots for eyes. Sew 9 mm jingle bell to tip of hat. Glue leaves beside beard at neck edge. Glue 6 mm red jingle bells over leaves for holly berries. Sew single loop of metallic thread through top seam of hat; bring ends of thread together and knot for hanging loop.

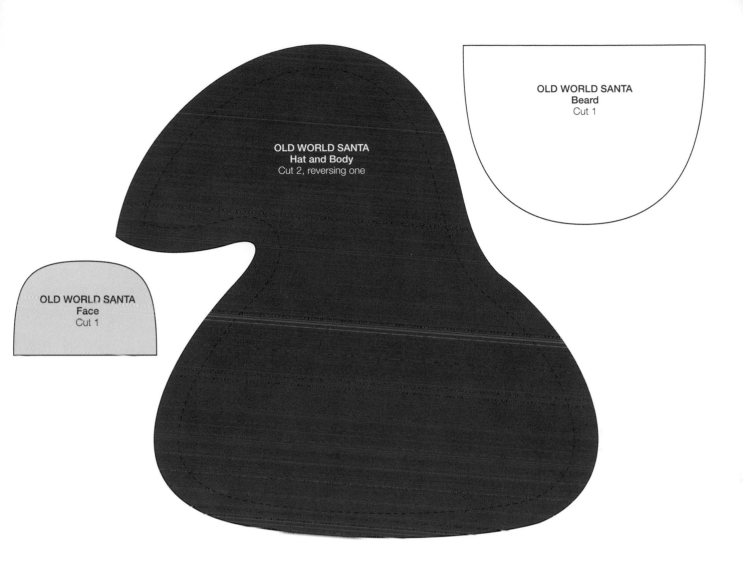

OLD WORLD SANTA
Hat and Body
Cut 2, reversing one

OLD WORLD SANTA
Beard
Cut 1

OLD WORLD SANTA
Face
Cut 1

Storing Christmas Trims and Ornaments

Because many Christmas decorations are fragile, proper and careful storage is important. Christmas items should be packed and safely stored during the year but well marked and easy to find for the holiday season. These tips will help keep your Christmas clutter organized and safe until you need it the following season.

Packing

Save large, sturdy cardboard boxes from previous Christmases for storing bulbs, ornaments, and lights. Boxes should be fairly shallow but large enough so that two or three boxes hold all of your tree ornaments. Mark the contents on the outside of each box, and fill the box with the same items from year to year. Time used packing the boxes carefully is well spent when it comes time to get out the ornaments for the next Christmas.

Storing

Designate an area in your basement, attic, or garage as Christmas storage. Use the same space every year so you will remember where to find your decorations. Position the boxes off the floor to keep out moisture. Clean the storage area thoroughly each year before returning decorations to storage. Mark areas where boxes are to be placed.

Wrap fragile bulbs and ornaments in tissue paper. Stack the remaining ornaments (from heavy to light) on layers of tissue paper or newspaper. Use angel hair and tinsel between the ornaments for added protection. Remove hooks and hangers from each ornament and store the hangers separately in a small box or envelope.

Check and replace burned-out bulbs before storing Christmas tree lights. To store, gather the lights carefully so they do not tangle.

Store your tree stand in its original box and include the tree skirt if there is enough room.

Spread holiday cheer throughout the house with centerpieces and displays that say "Merry Christmas!"

Create a clever **Christmas Under Glass** display, *above*, by using a simple birdbath for interest at a doorway or entry. Choose your favorite citrus fruits in pretty colors of green, yellow, and orange to arrange a **Carved Citrus Centerpiece,** *opposite*. For instructions, see page 110.

center of attention

Make a mantel or table sparkle by carving snowflakes in glass.
The **Etched Goblet Trio**, *opposite*, is made using a tiny drill and
simple snowflake patterns. Assemble a **Cranberry Candle**
Arrangement, *above*, in no time with a pillar candle and fresh
cranberries. For instructions see page 111.

One simple trick of using a smaller vase inside a larger one is all it takes to create all kinds of clever centerpieces. **Bright Blooms and Coffee Beans,** *opposite,* are arranged using a set of square vases. The **Pretty Nuts in Shells Centerpiece,** *above,* uses a hurricane-style vase with a smaller straight vase inside. A simple round vase is the container for a **Roses and Candy Centerpiece,** *below.* Instructions for all of the centerpieces are on pages 111–112.

Purchase a bloom in Christmas colors, add a white vase, and you will have a **Candy Cane Amaryllis Arrangement**, *right*. Little silver vases of all styles circle together to make a beautiful **Reflective Arrangement**, *below*. White hydrangeas and white candy canes combine for a stunning **Winter White Arrangement**, *opposite*. Instructions for all of the projects are on page 113.

Christmas Under Glass

Shown on page 102

WHAT YOU NEED

Purchased ceramic bird bath
Circle of glass to cover top of bird bath
Balls of moss (available in the floral
   department of discount stores)
Small ornaments
Small wrapped packages

HERE'S HOW

Set the bird bath where it will be
displayed. Fill with moss and ornaments.
Cover with the glass top. Add packages
on top of the glass.

Carved Citrus Centerpiece

Shown on page 103

WHAT YOU NEED

Fresh lemons, limes, and oranges
Small towel
Linoleum cutter with blades
Kitchen paint brush
Lemon juice; whole cloves
Glass compote; fresh greens

HERE'S HOW

Plan a design to carve into the outer layer
of the fruit. Choose simple lines to make
a tree shape, simple stars, or lines. Lay the
piece of fruit on the towel. Steady the
fruit with one hand and carefully, using
the linoleum tool, cut away from your
body. Be careful as linoleum tools are very
sharp. After carving the design, brush the
fruit with lemon juice. Then stick the

whole cloves into the design as desired.
Arrange in a glass compote and add fresh
greenery. The arrangement will last for
about 3 days unless refrigerated.

Etched Goblet Trio

Shown on page 104

WHAT YOU NEED

Tracing paper; pencil
Red glass stemware
Grease pencil or visaline marker
Protective eye covering
Old towel
Rotary tool such as Dremel with cable
Conical stone bit tool
Small votive cups
Tea light candles; ribbon

HERE'S HOW

1. Trace desired pattern, *opposite*, onto
tracing paper.
2. Sketch or draw pattern on glassware
with marker or grease pencil.
3. Place conical stone bit in cable
attachment. Put on protective eye
covering. Place glassware on folded towel.

4. Using tip of conical stone bit begin etching on lines of design. Use light pressure and try to move in fluid motions. Go over all lines (touching up where necessary) until entire design is on glass.
5. Clean glass thoroughly by washing with mild soap and water.
6. Insert votive holder and tea light into the stemware. Tie bow at base of each piece set in a line for centerpiece.

Never leave a burning candle unattended.

ETCHED GOBLET TRIO SNOWFLAKE PATTERNS

Cranberry Candle Arrangement
Shown on page 105

WHAT YOU NEED
Clear glass plate or small dish
Clear glass saucer or curved-edge dish
Pink or red pillar candle
Fresh cranberries

HERE'S HOW
Be sure the clear dishes are clean and dry. Place the saucer on the plate. Put the candle in the saucer. Arrange fresh cranberries in the saucer and on the plate.

Never leave a burning candle unattended.

Bright Blooms and Coffee Beans
Shown on page 106

WHAT YOU NEED
Small glass vase approximately the same height as the large vase
Larger square glass vase
Coffee beans
Long bamboo pick or kabob pick
Fresh blooms and bear grass or other greenery

HERE'S HOW
Place the small vase inside the larger vase to create a pocket for the coffee beans. Carefully fill the area between the vases with the coffee beans. Use the bamboo stick to adjust the beans. Fill the inside vase with water, fresh blooms, and pieces of bear grass that is looped back into the smaller vase or use other fresh greenery.

To add to the larger arrangement, use shorter vases as candleholders around the center arrangement. Place candles in into the smaller vases and surround them with coffee beans.

Small Christmas candies
Long bamboo pick or kabob pick
Roses and greenery

HERE'S HOW
Place the small vase inside the larger vase creating a pocket for the small candies. Carefully add the candies. Use the bamboo stick to adjust the candies as needed. Fill the inside vase with water and add the roses and greenery.

Pretty Nuts in Shells Centerpiece
Shown on page 107

WHAT YOU NEED
Small glass vase approximately the same height as the large vase
Larger hurricane-style vase
Mixed nuts in shells
Long bamboo pick or kabob pick
Dried or fresh blooms and greenery

HERE'S HOW
Place the smaller vase in the larger vase creating a pocket for the nuts. Carefully add the nuts between the two vases using the bamboo stick to adjust as needed. Fill the inside vase with blooms and greenery.

Roses and Candy Centerpiece
Shown on page 107

WHAT YOU NEED
Small glass vase approximately the same height as the large vase
Larger round glass vase

Reflective Arrangement
Shown on page 108

WHAT YOU NEED
Short silver vases in varied styles
Green hydrangeas
Mint julep
Green Christmas ornaments

HERE'S HOW
Arrange the vases in a circle in the center of the table. Fill with water. Cut the hydrangeas short and put in the vases. Tuck in pieces of mint julep and green Christmas ornaments.

Candy Cane Amaryllis Arrangement
Shown on page 108

WHAT YOU NEED
Candy Cane Amaryllis
White vase; white tray
Small wrapped package

HERE'S HOW
Cut the amaryllis and place in the vase. Place on the tray. Add a small white package wrapped in red ribbon at the bottom of the vase.

Winter White Arrangement
Shown on page 109

WHAT YOU NEED
White hydrangeas
Scissors
Green vase or urn
Fresh greenery
White candy canes
Pink and green ornaments

HERE'S HOW
Cut the hydrangeas to fit into the container. Fill the container with water. Place the cut hydrangeas in the container. Add the fresh greenery, ornaments, and candy canes in the center of the arrangement.

teatime treats

When jam-packed holiday calendars make a weekend-night gathering all but impossible, your friends will appreciate it when you say, "Come for tea!" It is a cheerful way to gather, especially when these well-chosen treats are part of the merrymaking.

Invite friends to pop in for tea after a long day of shopping.

They will feel fortified and refreshed when you serve a strong "cuppa"

with **Roast Beef Tea Sandwiches with Horseradish Cream** and

Ribbon Sandwiches, *opposite,* as well as rich **White Chocolate-Apricot**

Mini Scones, *above.* Recipes are on page 121.

Here are three lavish takes on tea cakes—all in cute mini-versions that are perfect for sampling a great array of flavors. **Dried Fruit Tea Cakes,** *below,* are tasty and traditional, while **Peach-Rum Babas,** *above,* and **Phyllo Stacks with Cranberry-Cream Filling,** *opposite,* bring new tastes to the teatime table. Recipes are on pages 122–123.

Make Christmas tea complete with colorful cookies to nibble and dunk. For a honey of a take on the holiday cutout cookie, try **Honey-Butter Cookies,** *opposite.* **Lemon and Poppy Seed Cornmeal Cookies,** *below left,* taste so irresistible they need no frosting. Sprinkle a little sugarplum magic throughout **Elfin Shortbread Bites,** *below right.* Recipes are on page 124.

Rely on these striking sweets to pretty-up your buffet table. **Maple-and-Chestnut Mincemeat Tarts,** *above,* combine two time-honored flavors in one luscious treat. **Citrus Pound Cake Tea Cakes,** *below,* are easy because they start with a purchased pound cake. Recipes are on page 125.

Roast Beef Tea Sandwiches with Horseradish Cream

Shown on page 114

WHAT YOU NEED

2 tablespoons dairy sour cream
1 teaspoon prepared horseradish
½ teaspoon snipped fresh chives
   Kosher salt
   Ground black pepper
1 tablespoon butter, softened
4 slices thinly sliced firm-textured rye or marbled sandwich bread
4 thin, deli-style slices cooked roast beef (5 ounces)
   Thinly sliced radishes or small pickles

HERE'S HOW

1. In a small bowl combine sour cream, horseradish, and chives. Season with salt and pepper.
2. Spread butter on one side of each slice of bread. Spread 2 of the buttered slices with horseradish mixture. Top with roast beef. Top with remaining bread slices, buttered side down. Trim the crusts from bread. Cut each sandwich diagonally into 2 triangles. Top each with radish slices and/or small pickles speared on toothpicks before serving. Makes 4 appetizer sandwiches.
Make-Ahead Directions: Place prepared sandwiches on a plate. Cover tightly with plastic wrap and chill in the refrigerator for up to 1 hour before serving.

Ribbon Sandwiches

Shown on page 114

WHAT YOU NEED

3 hard-cooked eggs, peeled and finely chopped (see Note, page 81)
4 teaspoons mayonnaise or salad dressing
1 tablespoon finely chopped green onion
½ teaspoon sugar
   Salt and ground black pepper
2 tablespoons mayonnaise or salad dressing
½ of a 3-ounce package cream cheese, softened
¼ cup chopped pimiento-stuffed green olives or pitted ripe olives
2 tablespoons finely chopped toasted nuts
2 tablespoons butter, softened
5 slices thin-sliced white bread, crusts removed
4 slices thin-sliced whole wheat bread, crusts removed
   Pimiento-stuffed green olives and/or cherry tomato wedges (optional)

HERE'S HOW

1. For egg filling, in a small bowl combine eggs, 4 teaspoons mayonnaise, green onion, sugar, and salt and pepper to taste. Cover and chill while preparing other filling.
2. For olive-nut filling, in a small bowl beat the 2 tablespoons mayonnaise and the cream cheese together until combined. Add the chopped olives and nuts; stir gently until just combined.
3. To assemble, butter one side of each slice of bread. On a cutting board, lay 2 slices of white bread and 1 slice of whole wheat bread.
4. Spread egg filling on each. Top the 2 filled white bread slices with a whole wheat slice and the filled whole wheat slice with a white slice. Spread with olive-nut filling. Top with remaining bread slices, white on whole-wheat-filled and whole wheat slice on white-filled slice. Cover and chill sandwiches for 2 to 4 hours. Slice each sandwich crosswise into thirds. If desired, garnish with olives, and/or tomato wedges speared on toothpicks. Makes 9 appetizers.

White Chocolate-Apricot Mini Scones

Shown on page 115

WHAT YOU NEED

½ cup finely snipped dried apricots
2 cups all-purpose flour
2 tablespoons granulated sugar
1 tablespoon baking powder
½ teaspoon salt
⅓ cup butter
½ cup whipping cream
1 egg, beaten
1 teaspoon vanilla
4 ounces white chocolate, coarsely shredded
   Whipping cream
   Coarse sugar

HERE'S HOW

1. Preheat oven to 400°F. Place apricots in a small bowl; add enough boiling water to cover. Let soak for 5 minutes; drain well. In a large bowl combine flour, 2 tablespoons sugar, the baking powder, and salt. Using a pastry blender, cut in butter until mixture resembles coarse crumbs. Make a well in the center of the flour mixture; set mixture aside.
2. In a medium bowl combine ½ cup whipping cream, the egg, and vanilla. Stir in the drained apricots and chocolate. Add the egg mixture all at once to flour mixture. Using a fork, stir just until moistened.
3. Turn dough out onto a lightly floured surface. Knead dough by folding and gently pressing it for 10 to 12 strokes or until dough is nearly smooth. Pat or lightly roll dough until ¾-inch thick. Using a well floured 1¼- to 1½-inch round cutter, cut out dough, rerolling scraps as necessary and dipping cutter into flour between cuts.
4. Place dough circles 2 inches apart on large ungreased baking sheets. Brush circles with additional whipping cream and sprinkle with coarse sugar. Bake for 10 to 12 minutes or until tops are golden. Remove scones from baking sheet; serve warm. Makes 45 mini scones.
To store: Place scones in an airtight container. Cover and store at room temperature for up to 3 days or freeze for up to 1 month.

Peach-Rum Babas

Shown on page 116

WHAT YOU NEED

- ½ cup butter
- 2 eggs
  Nonstick cooking spray for baking
- 1 cup all-purpose flour
- ¾ teaspoon baking powder
- ⅛ teaspoon ground nutmeg
- ½ cup granulated sugar
- 3 tablespoons peach liqueur
- ½ teaspoon finely shredded
  lemon peel or orange peel
- ½ teaspoon vanilla
- ⅓ cup granulated sugar
- ¼ cup water
- 2 tablespoons packed brown sugar
- 2 tablespoons light-colored
  corn syrup
- ¼ cup rum or amaretto
  Whipped cream
  Assorted fresh berries

HERE'S HOW

1. Let butter and eggs stand at room temperature for 30 minutes. Meanwhile, generously coat six ¾-cup miniature fluted tube pans with nonstick cooking spray for baking (or grease and flour the pans). In a small bowl combine flour, baking powder, and nutmeg; set aside.

2. Preheat oven to 325°F. In a large mixing bowl beat butter with an electric mixer on medium to high speed for 30 seconds. Add the ½ cup granulated sugar, 2 tablespoons at a time, beating on medium-high speed about 6 minutes or until mixture is very light and fluffy.

3. Stir in peach liqueur, lemon peel, and vanilla. Add eggs, one at a time, beating for 1 minute after each addition and scraping bowl frequently. Gradually add flour mixture to egg mixture, beating on medium-low speed just until combined. Pour into prepared pans.

4. Bake for 20 to 25 minutes or until a wooden toothpick inserted near the centers comes out clean. Cool in pans on wire racks for 10 minutes. Remove from pans; cool on wire racks, fluted sides up. Prick the fluted top and side of each cake generously with the tines of a fork.

5. For syrup, in a medium saucepan combine the ⅓ cup granulated sugar, the water, brown sugar, and corn syrup. Cook and stir over medium heat until syrup is bubbly and most of the sugar is dissolved; remove from heat. Stir in rum. Cool for 5 minutes.

6. Dip the top half of each cooled cake into syrup. Place cakes on wire racks above a large tray or baking sheet. Spoon or brush any remaining syrup over cakes. Cool cakes completely on wire racks. Serve cakes topped with whipped cream and berries. Makes 6 servings.

Make-Ahead Directions: Prepare as directed, except do not garnish with whipped cream and berries. Wrap cooled cakes individually in plastic wrap. Chill, fluted sides up, in the refrigerator for up to 3 days. Serve with whipped cream and berries.

Dried Fruit Tea Cakes

Shown on page 116

WHAT YOU NEED

- 1 cup golden raisins
- 1 cup dried cranberries or
  dried tart cherries
- ½ cup bourbon or apple cider
  Nonstick cooking spray
- 1¾ cups all-purpose flour
- 1½ teaspoons baking powder
- ¼ teaspoon salt
- ⅔ cup butter, softened
- 1 cup sugar
- 2 eggs
- ⅔ cup milk
- 1 recipe Bourbon or Cider Drizzle
  Candied orange peel (optional)

HERE'S HOW

1. In a small bowl combine fruit and bourbon. Cover; let stand 1 hour. Drain fruit, reserving the liquid for the Bourbon Drizzle. Preheat oven to 350°F. Lightly coat desired pans with cooking spray (see pan sizes in chart, *opposite below*).

2. In a medium bowl stir together flour, baking powder, and salt. In a large mixing bowl beat butter with an electric mixer on medium to high speed for 30 seconds. Add sugar and beat until fluffy.

3. Add eggs, one at a time, to butter mixture, beating well after each addition. Alternately add the dry ingredients and milk to butter mixture, beating well after each addition. Stir in drained fruit.

4. Spread batter in prepared pans. Bake until a wooden toothpick inserted in center comes out clean (see baking times in chart, *below*). Cool in pans on wire rack for 10 minutes; remove from pans. Spoon on Bourbon Drizzle. If desired, top with candied orange peel. Cool on wire rack. Makes 13 mini loaves, 9 medium loaves, 1 large loaf, or 24 cupcakes.

Bourbon or Cider Drizzle: Measure reserved soaking liquid; add water to equal ½ cup. In a small saucepan combine 1 teaspoon sugar and ½ teaspoon cornstarch; add liquid. Cook and stir until thickened and bubbly; cook and stir 2 minutes more. Cool 10 minutes; spoon over cakes. Makes about ⅔ cup.

Phyllo Stacks with Cranberry-Cream Filling

Shown on page 117

WHAT YOU NEED

- 4 sheets frozen phyllo dough (14×9-inch rectangles), thawed
- ⅓ cup butter, melted
- ⅓ cup granulated sugar
- 1 3-ounce package cream cheese, softened
- ¼ cup dairy sour cream
- ¼ teaspoon vanilla
  Dash ground cinnamon
  Dash ground nutmeg
- ½ cup powdered sugar
- ¼ cup snipped dried cranberries or dried cherries
- ½ teaspoon finely shredded orange peel or lemon peel
- ¼ cup cherry preserves
- 1 recipe Candied Orange Peel Strips (optional)
  Coarse sugar (optional)

HERE'S HOW

1. Preheat oven to 375°F. Line a large baking sheet with foil; set aside.

2. For phyllo stack, unfold phyllo dough and remove 1 sheet. (As you work, keep the remaining phyllo dough covered with plastic wrap to prevent it from drying out.) Brush with some of the melted butter, being sure to brush it all the way to the edges. Sprinkle with some of the granulated sugar. Place a second sheet of phyllo on top of the first; brush with butter and sprinkle with granulated sugar. Repeat with remaining 2 phyllo sheets, brushing each one with butter and sprinkling with granulated sugar.

3. Cut the phyllo stack crosswise into 8 strips (each about 1¾ inches wide). Cut each strip into thirds to make 24 rectangles total (each about 3×1¾ inches). Place the rectangles on the prepared baking sheet. Bake for 6 to 8 minutes or until lightly browned (phyllo will crisp as it cools). Transfer to a wire rack; cool completely.

4. For filling, in a medium mixing bowl combine cream cheese, sour cream, vanilla, cinnamon, and nutmeg. Beat with an electric mixer on medium speed until smooth. Beat in the powdered sugar. Stir in cranberries and shredded orange peel.

5. To assemble each stack, spread about 1 tablespoon of the filling on each of 12 baked phyllo rectangles. Snip any large pieces of fruit in the preserves. Spread about 1 teaspoon of the preserves on each filled phyllo rectangle.

6. If desired, garnish remaining phyllo rectangles with Candied Orange Peel Strips formed into bow shapes and a sprinkle of coarse sugar. Place the garnished phyllo rectangles on the preserve-topped phyllo rectangles to make 12 stacks. Chill for at least 30 minutes or up to 2½ hours. Makes 12 stacks.

Candied Orange Peel Strips: Cut peels of 2 oranges lengthwise into quarters, cutting just through the pulp to the surface of the fruit. Pry back the quartered peel using the back of a spoon. Using the bowl of the spoon, scrape away the soft white part inside the peel (pith). Cut peel into strips. In a 2-quart saucepan combine 1⅓ cups granulated sugar and ⅓ cup water. Cover and bring to boiling. Add orange peel strips. Return to boiling, stirring constantly to dissolve sugar. Reduce heat. Cook, uncovered, over medium-low heat. Mixture should boil at a moderate, steady rate over entire surface. Cook, stirring occasionally, for 15 minutes or until strips are almost translucent. Remove from heat. Using a slotted spoon, remove strips from syrup, allowing each spoonful to drain over the saucepan about 30 seconds. Transfer peel to a wire rack set over waxed paper. Set cooked peel aside until cool enough to handle but still warm and slightly sticky. Roll strips in coarse sugar or granulated sugar. Continue drying on the rack for 1 to 2 hours. Makes about 2 cups peel.

Make-Ahead Directions: Prepare the phyllo stacks as above through Step 3. Place in an airtight container and store at room temperature for up to 1 day. Prepare filling in Step 4. Store in a covered container in the refrigerator for up to 1 day. Prepare Candied Orange Peel Strips; store in a tightly covered container in a cool, dry place for up to 1 week or in the freezer for up to 6 months. To assemble, continue with Steps 5 and 6. Chill at least 30 minutes or up to 2½ hours.

Choose Your Pan for Dried Fruit Tea Cakes

Lightly coat with nonstick cooking spray or grease and flour the bottom and ½ inch up the sides of loaf pans or muffin cups.

PAN SIZE	BATTER AMOUNT	TIME	YIELD
3¼×2¼×1¼-inch	⅓ cup	18 to 20 minutes	13
4½×2½×1½-inch	½ cup	18 to 20 minutes	9
9×5×3-inch	entire recipe	1 hour	1
2½-inch muffin cups	3 tablespoons	15 minutes	24

Honey-Butter Cookies

Shown on page 118

WHAT YOU NEED

⅓ cup butter, softened
⅓ cup granulated sugar
1 teaspoon baking soda
¼ teaspoon salt
⅔ cup honey
1 egg
½ teaspoon lemon extract (optional)
2¾ cups all-purpose flour
1 recipe Honey-Butter Frosting
Small candies

HERE'S HOW

1. In a large mixing bowl beat butter with an electric mixer on medium to high speed for 30 seconds. Add sugar, baking soda, and salt. Beat until combined, scraping sides of bowl occasionally. Beat in honey, egg, and if desired, lemon extract, until combined. Beat in as much of the flour as you can with the mixer. Stir in any remaining flour with a wooden spoon. Cover dough and chill for 1 hour or until dough is easy to handle.
2. Preheat oven to 375°F. Lightly grease a cookie sheet; set aside. On a lightly floured surface, roll dough until ⅛ to ¼ inch thick. Using 2½-inch cookie cutters, cut dough into desired shapes. Place cutouts 1 inch apart on prepared cookie sheet.
3. Bake for 7 to 8 minutes or until cookies are golden and edges are set. Transfer to a wire rack and let cool.

To decorate, use a decorating bag fitted with a plain round tip to pipe Honey-Butter Frosting on cooled cookies and trim as desired with small candies. Makes about 30 cookies.
Honey-Butter Frosting: In a medium saucepan combine 3 tablespoons butter and 3 tablespoons honey; bring to boiling. Remove from heat. Stir in 2 cups powdered sugar and 2 teaspoons lemon juice. Cool to room temperature. If necessary, stir in milk, 1 teaspoon at a time, until frosting is of spreading consistency. Divide frosting into 3 portions and tint one-third with red food coloring and one-third with green food coloring. Leave one-third white.
To store: Place cookies in layers separated by waxed paper in an airtight container; cover. Store at room temperature for up to 3 days or freeze unfrosted cookies for up to 1 month. Thaw cookies; frost.

Lemon and Poppy Seed Cornmeal Cookies

Shown on page 119

WHAT YOU NEED

1 8.5 ounce package corn muffin mix
½ cup quick-cooking rolled oats
¼ cup sugar
2 tablespoons butter, softened
1 egg, lightly beaten
2 teaspoons milk
1 teaspoon finely shredded lemon peel
1 teaspoon poppy seeds

HERE'S HOW

1. Preheat oven to 375°F. Line a cookie sheet with parchment paper; set aside. In a medium bowl stir together corn muffin mix, oats, sugar, butter, egg, milk, lemon peel, and poppy seeds until combined. Drop dough by level measuring teaspoons 2 inches apart onto the prepared cookie sheet.
2. Bake for 7 to 9 minutes or until lightly browned. Transfer to a wire rack and let cool. Makes about 60 cookies.
To store: Place cookies in layers separated by waxed paper in an airtight container; cover. Store at room temperature for up to 3 days or freeze for up to 3 months.

Elfin Shortbread Bites

Shown on page 119

WHAT YOU NEED

1¼ cups all-purpose flour
3 tablespoons sugar
½ cup butter
2 tablespoons colored sprinkles

HERE'S HOW

1. Preheat oven to 325°F. In a medium bowl stir together flour and sugar. Using a pastry blender, cut in butter until mixture resembles fine crumbs and starts to cling. Stir in colored sprinkles. Form mixture into a ball and knead until smooth.
2. Roll or pat dough on an ungreased cookie sheet into an 8×5-inch rectangle. Cut into ½-inch squares. Separate the squares on the cookie sheet.

3. Bake for 12 to 14 minutes or until the bottoms just start to brown. Transfer to wire racks covered with waxed paper to cool. Makes about 160 tiny cookies.
To store: Place cooled cookie bites in a tightly covered container. Store at room temperature for up to 3 days or in the freezer for up to 3 months.

Maple-and-Chestnut Mincemeat Tarts
Shown on page 120

WHAT YOU NEED
- 1 cup butter, softened
- 1 8-ounce package cream cheese, softened
- 2¼ cups all-purpose flour
- ¼ teaspoon ground allspice or ground cinnamon
- 2 eggs
- ¾ cup packed brown sugar
- ¼ cup pure maple syrup or maple-flavor syrup
- ¾ cup purchased mincemeat
- ½ cup canned whole, peeled chestnuts, drained and chopped, or canned candied chestnuts, drained and chopped
  Powdered sugar (optional)
  Cut-up candied cherries and dried apricots (optional)

HERE'S HOW
1. Preheat oven to 325°F. For pastry, in a large mixing bowl beat butter and cream cheese with an electric mixer on medium to high speed for 30 seconds. Stir in flour and allspice. Divide dough in half. Wrap one portion of dough and chill in the refrigerator until needed. Press a rounded teaspoon of remaining dough evenly into bottom and up the sides of 24 ungreased 1¾-inch muffin cups.
2. For filling, in a medium bowl beat eggs, brown sugar, and maple syrup until combined. Stir in mincemeat and chopped chestnuts. Divide filling in half. Cover one portion of filling with plastic wrap; chill in the refrigerator until needed. Spoon about 1 heaping teaspoon of remaining filling into each pastry-lined muffin cup.
3. Bake tarts for 25 to 30 minutes or until pastry is golden and filling puffs. Cool slightly in pan. Carefully transfer to a wire rack; cool. Repeat with remaining pastry and filling.
4. If desired, hold a fork over each tart and sprinkle with sifted powdered sugar, making a stenciled design. If desired, top with pieces of candied cherry and dried apricot. Makes 48 tarts.
To Store: Place tarts in layers separated by waxed paper in an airtight container; cover. Store at room temperature for up to 3 days or freeze for up to 3 months.

Citrus Pound Cake Tea Cakes
Shown on page 120

WHAT YOU NEED
- 1 3-ounce package cream cheese, softened
- 1 teaspoon orange juice
- ¼ cup powdered sugar
- 1 teaspoon finely shredded lemon peel
- ½ teaspoon finely shredded orange peel
- ¼ cup finely chopped pecans, toasted
- 1 10.75-ounce frozen pound cake, thawed
- ¼ cup orange marmalade
- ¼ cup flaked coconut, toasted

HERE'S HOW
1. For filling, in a small mixing bowl beat cream cheese and orange juice with an electric mixer on medium speed until smooth. Beat in powdered sugar. Stir in ½ teaspoon of the lemon peel and the orange peel until combined. Stir in pecans. Set filling aside.
2. Trim the crust from the thawed pound cake. Cut the cake crosswise into 12 slices. Spread the cream cheese filling over half of the slices. Top with the remaining slices.
3. Cut each diagonally in half. In a small saucepan melt marmalade over low heat. Stir in remaining ½ teaspoon lemon peel. Brush marmalade over the tops of the triangles. Sprinkle each with toasted coconut, pressing gently so it sticks. Makes 6 servings.
Make-Ahead Directions: Prepare as directed through Step 2. Cover and chill in the refrigerator for up to 4 hours. Before serving, continue with Step 3.

wreaths all around

Whether you love glorious holiday wreaths of silver and gold or simple wreaths with happy snowman faces and paper snowflakes—create a perfect wreath to welcome your holiday visitors.

A **Holiday Table Wreath,** *above,* is easy to make and takes you through the holidays in style. Pinecones and ornaments combine to make this inviting **Copper Luster Pinecone Wreath,** *opposite.* The pinecones are wired on the wreath, dusted with copper and cranberry color, and wrapped in pretty ribbon. Instructions are on page 134.

Vegetables and fruits combine in an unexpected fashion to make an elegant green **Veggie Lover's Wreath,** *above,* to hang outside in the cool winter air. Fresh or artificial roses and fresh lily grass bring new flair to red and green in a **Roses and Lily Grass Wreath,** *opposite above.* Make a clever **Starstruck Wreath,** *opposite below,* in no time using a fresh green wreath and silver accents. Instructions for all of the wreaths are on pages 135–136.

Show your holiday best with a **Vintage Sparkle Wreath**, *above*, using costume jewelry and a luxurious satin bow. If you don't have enough jewelry, use inexpensive pearls and faux jewels from the crafts store. Overlap die-cut snowflakes from a scrapbook store to make a wintery **Paper Snowflake Wreath**, *opposite above*. Shades of deep velvety blues and greens bestow quiet beauty to a **Cool Winter Wreath**, *opposite below*, made of Aspidistra leaves and small ornaments. Instructions for the wreaths are on pages 136–137.

Make a **Happy Snowman Wreath,** *above right,* by stitching up a soft snowman with his own hat and scarf. Add a pair of gloves and snowballs to complete the clever door wreath. For that fanatic fisherman, make a playful **Fish Bobber Wreath,** *below right.* Perfect for an informal family room, this bright wreath will bring smiles. Just look outside for ideas to use in a **Natural Touch Wreath,** *opposite.* This one comes together with handfuls of fresh curly willow branches and red dogwood. Bright red cardinals and red-hue ornaments complete the becoming wreath. Instructions for all of the wreaths are on pages 138–139.

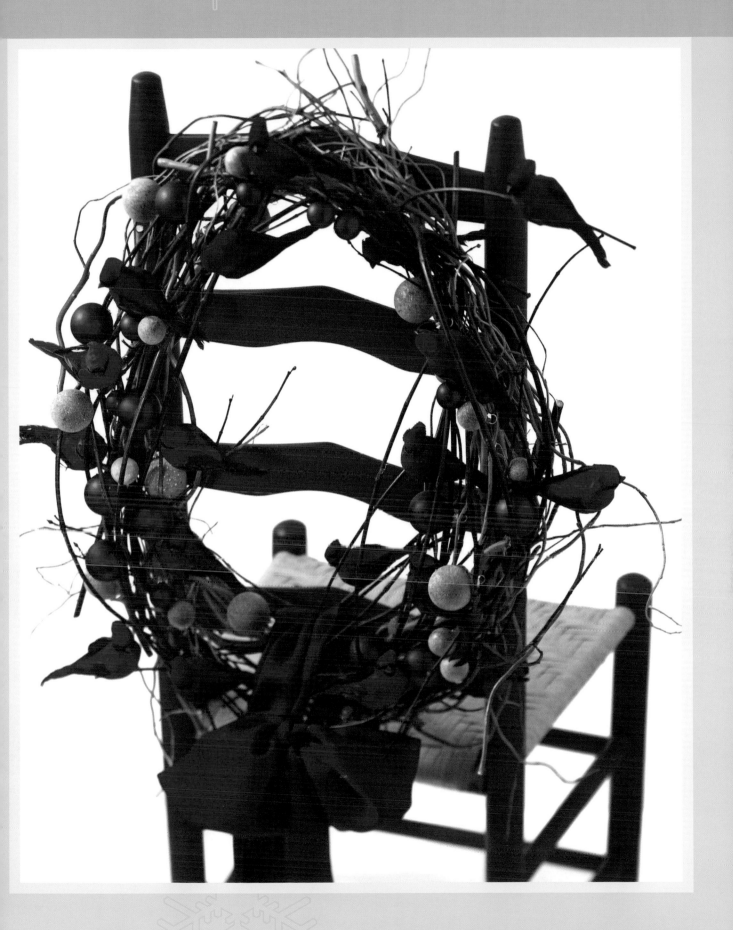

HERE'S HOW

Be sure the pinecones are clean and dry. Wire the back of each pinecone leaving about 6 inches of wire to attach to the wreath form. After wiring all of the pinecones, start wiring them to the form placing the larger ones first and adding the smaller ones around the larger ones. Fill in the entire wreath with pinecones. Add a wire to the back for hanging. Lay the wreath on a covered surface and spray with copper spray paint. Let dry. Lightly spray over the copper color with cranberry spray paint. Let dry. Wrap the gold ribbon loosely around the wreath securing in the back. Tie a bow with the cranberry ribbon and wire to the top of the wreath. Wire on the leaf ornaments.

Holiday Table Wreath

Shown on page 127

WHAT YOU NEED

Pinecones
Fine wire
Wire snips or old scissors
Purchased grapevine wreath
Dried flowers in desired colors
Cake plate
Clear glass light shade
Votive candle

Copper Luster Pinecone Wreath

Shown on page 126

WHAT YOU NEED

About 50 pinecones in all sizes
   and styles
Fine wire
Wire snips or old scissors
16-inch wreath form
Copper spray paint
Cranberry-red spray paint
½-inch-wide gold ribbon
3-inch-wide cranberry ribbon
Purchased leaf-shaped ornaments

HERE'S HOW

Wire the pinecones by wrapping the fine wire around one end of the pinecone. Wire the pinecones to the wreath. Place dried flowers between the pinecones in a random fashion. Place the wreath on the cake plate. Invert the glass shade in the middle of the wreath. Place the votive candle in the center of the glass shade.

Never leave a burning candle unattended.

Veggie Lover's Wreath
Shown on page 128

WHAT YOU NEED
Foam wreath form
Variety of small green fruits and
    vegetables such as Brussel
    sprouts, grapes, artichokes, limes,
    asparagus, etc.
Fine greenery
Small green ornaments
Fine wire; wire snips or old scissors

Long pins; floral picks
3 yards of lime green satin ribbon

HERE'S HOW
Lay the foam wreath on a covered surface. Cut the vegetables and practice arranging them on the form. After the arrangement is decided, attach the fruits and vegetables with wire, long pins, and floral picks. Fill gaps by wiring in greenery and small ornaments. Tie a bow and add to the top of the wreath. *Note:* This wreath is best displayed on an outside door in cool weather. This wreath will last outside in cold weather for about 4 days. The wreath will spoil more rapidly if kept indoors.

Roses and Lily Grass Wreath
Shown on page 129

WHAT YOU NEED
Fresh "hocus pocus" (yellow and red)
    roses or artificial roses

Oasis foam wreath
Water in shallow dish if using
    fresh flowers
Lily grass
Straight pins
Juniper sprigs
Matte-finish ornaments
Fine wire
Wire snips or old scissors
Ribbon bow

HERE'S HOW
If using fresh flowers, soak the foam wreath in shallow dish until it is moist but not dripping with water. Lay the foam wreath on a covered surface. Clip the tops from the roses and poke the ends into the wreath. Wrap the lily grass around the wreath and secure with pins in the back. Poke the juniper sprigs into the wreath. Wire the ornaments and poke into the wreath. Add a bow if desired. *Note:* Fresh flowers will keep in this wreath for about 2 days.

Star Struck Wreath
Shown on page 129

WHAT YOU NEED
Purchased fresh evergreen wreath
Silver paint
Paint brush
Silver chenille stems
Wire
Wire snips or old scissors
Purchased garland of silver beads
Precut wood star shapes (available
  at crafts stores)

HERE'S HOW
1. Paint the wood stars silver. Let dry.
Wire each star so it can be attached to
the wreath. Set aside.
2. Poke the silver chenille stems into
the evergreen on the wreath.
3. Wrap the garland loosely around the
wreath. Wire the stars into the wreath.

Vintage Sparkle Wreath
Shown on page 130

WHAT YOU NEED
16-inch foam wreath form
  such as Styrofoam
1 yard of 1-inch-wide
  cream-colored ribbon
Long straight pins
Vintage jewelry
Cream colored satin ribbon
Hot glue

HERE'S HOW
1. Lay the foam wreath on a flat surface.
Wrap the wreath with white ribbon and
pin to secure.
2. Arrange the jewelry on the ribbon.
3. Hot glue or pin in place. Wind pearls
or strings of jewelry over the secured
pieces of jewelry.

4. Tie a bow using the satin ribbon. Glue
or pin in place. Add another piece of
jewelry to the bow if desired.

Paper Snowflake Wreath
Shown on page 131

WHAT YOU NEED
Foam wreath form such as Styrofoam
  or cardboard wreath form
Dark blue spray paint
Purchased paper die-cut snowflakes
  (available at scrapbook stores)
Hot glue gun and glue sticks
Wire
Wire snips or old scissors

HERE'S HOW

Choose a foam or cardboard wreath form to fit the size of the purchased snowflakes. Spray paint the form dark blue. Let dry. Arrange the snowflakes on the form overlapping the snowflakes to make an interesting arrangement. Hot glue in place. Use wire to create a hanger for the back of the wreath.

Cool Winter Wreath

Shown on page 131

WHAT YOU NEED

Foam wreath form
Aspidistra leaves
Small bowl of warm water
Floral picks
Small blue, green, and white
    Christmas ornaments
Teal blue satin ribbon
Fine wire
Wire snips or old scissors

HERE'S HOW

Lay the wreath form on a flat surface. *Note:* To make the leaves bend nicely, lay them in the warm water while working. Bend the leaves and pin on the wreath form overlapping as you work. Cover the wreath with the leaves. Wire the ornaments and pin between and on the leaves. Tie a bow with the teal ribbon and pin to the top of the wreath. Add a cluster of small ornaments on top of the bow. Form a hanger from wire and attach it to the top back of the wreath.

Happy Snowman Wreath
Shown on page 132

WHAT YOU NEED
Tracing paper
Pencil; scissors
10-inch square of white fleece
Scrap orange fleece or felt
18-inch straw wreath
Sharp knife or hand saw
⅛ yard fleece fabric
Polyfil stuffing
Two ¾-inch black shank buttons
Five ⅜-inch black shank buttons
Two ⅝-inch shirt buttons
Two 15×30-inch pieces of plaid
    cotton fabric or flannel
Black felt party hat
Sprig artificial greenery and holly berries
One-size-fits-all lightweight knit
    gloves or mittens
Fabric glue
Long sewing pins
Matching threads

HERE'S HOW
1. Trace patterns, *right*. Cut head and nose from fleece fabrics. Stitch around outside rounded edges of head, using ½-inch seam allowance, leaving an opening for turning. Trim seam allowance

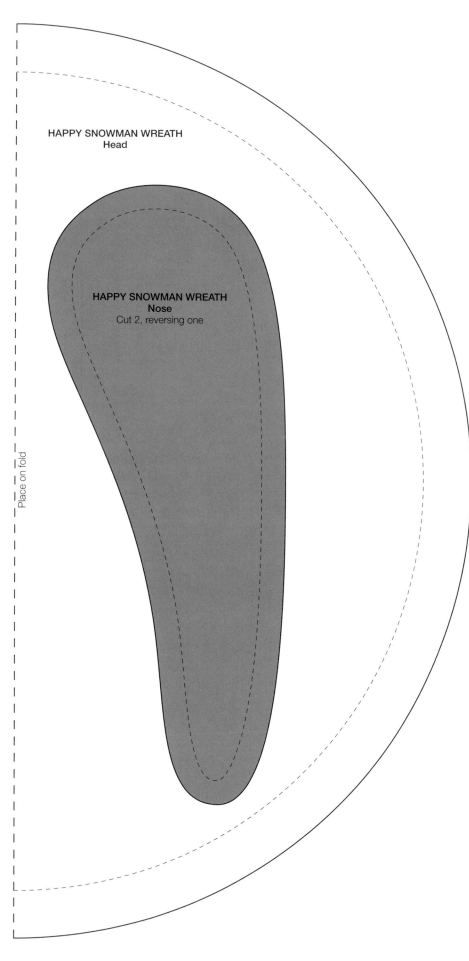

HAPPY SNOWMAN WREATH
Head

Place on fold

HAPPY SNOWMAN WREATH
Nose
Cut 2, reversing one

and clip all around curves. Turn, stuff with polyfil and sew opening closed using matching thread and small hand stitches. Prepare the nose in the same manner, using ¼-inch seam allowance. Sew nose to center of snowman face, using matching orange thread and taking small hand stitches to sew through nose and top layer of face fabric. Position larger ¾-inch black buttons for eyes and sew in place using black thread. Sew on smaller ⅜-inch black buttons for mouth.

2. With right sides together, sew short ends of plaid fabric together in ¼-inch seam. Press flat. With right sides together, stitch long edges of plaid fabric together to make a tube 7¼×60 inches long. At raw edges on ends of tube, fold 2½ inches to the inside and press. Stitch close to raw edges. Fold back the folded edge to make a 2-inch simulated shirt cuff. Set aside.

3. Cut wreath in half by making one slice with a sharp knife or hand saw. Cut hat in half with scissors. Glue greenery to one side of hat at the hatband. Cut fleece for scarf to 4½×54 inches. At both short ends, make cuts every ¼ inch, 3 inches in from ends for fringe.

4. Put sleeve tube around the wreath, sliding plaid fabric over the cut opening and moving it around to the other cut edge. Work stuffing loosely along top edge of wreath to puff out sleeves. Overlap cuffs at lower edges to fit tightly to wreath and to simulate a sleeve placket. Pin in place. Sew sleeve buttons through all layers of the overlap to secure. Lightly stuff fingers and thumbs of gloves with polyfil. Place gloves over cut ends of wreath and lightly stuff tops over wreath.

5. Hang wreath over a doorknob so that face can be positioned at top center of wreath. Push pins through edge of face and through wreath to hold in place. Using white thread secure head to several places around the wreath, hand stitching through top wrapping of wreath, plaid fabric, and fleece from the face piece. Position hat over head and tack in place with hand stitches at ends of hat, through plaid fabric, and top wrapping of wreath.

6. Wrap scarf around bottom of face and knot at side. Tack scarf to sides of wreath with hand stitches in the same manner.

Note: Wreath may be constructed using a purchased stocking cap instead of the black top hat. A secondhand flannel shirt may be cut to use the sleeves instead of the plaid fabric. If using a shirt instead of purchased fabric for the sleeves, measure the length of the sleeves and adjust the wreath accordingly to make sure sleeves reach around the entire wreath.

Fish Bobber Wreath

Shown on page 132

WHAT YOU NEED

12-inch wire wreath form
100-light-string of white lights
Spool of silver craft wire (21 gauge)
Assorted bobbers: ½ inch (24),
    ¾ inch (18), 1 inch (30), 1¼ inch (42),
    1½ inch (6), 1¾ inch (6) and
    2 inches (8). Note: These are
    approximate amounts depending
    on how they are arranged.
Needle-nose pliers; side wire cutters
3 yards of 3-inch-wide red, white,
    and green striped ribbon

HERE'S HOW

1. Wrap wreath form with the white light string, leaving plug free.
2. Fold 6-inch pieces of craft wire and hook bobber at fold. Place largest bobbers first, second largest next and so on.

3. Wire to wreath form, twisting wires to snag bobber and adjusting and positioning lights between bobbers. Cut wires and tuck ends.
4. Fill in with small bobbers and pull lights into place until wreath is full.
5. Make a large bow and add to the top of the wreath. Add a hanger wire to the back of wreath.

Natural Touch Wreath

Shown on page 133

WHAT YOU NEED

Curly willow branches
Red dogwood branches
Fine wire
Wire snips or old scissors
Hot glue gun and glue sticks
Artificial red cardinals
Small ornaments in red hues
2½-inch-wide red ribbon

HERE'S HOW

Wrap the branches to make a wreath shape. Secure with wire if necessary. Hot glue ornaments and birds to the wreath shape. Add a bow with red ribbon at the bottom of the wreath.

handmade gifts and greetings

Whether you like to paint, sew, knit, scrapbook, quilt, or assemble surprises in clever wraps, make this year special by presenting everyone on your Christmas list with a handmade gift or greeting.

A **Christmas Mailbox**, *opposite,* makes a clever and festive holder for all of the cards and greetings that come at Christmas time. Design one for yourself and then make some for friends and family. Just paint a tin mailbox and cover with scrapbook paper trims in colors that suit any decorating scheme. For instructions see page 151.

Merry Memories

Venture beyond baskets to discover containers to hold wonderful groupings of gifts. Gather gifts together in a pretty crock bowl for a **Comfort Food Crock with Apron,** *opposite above.* Make a **Fun and Games Box,** *opposite below,* full of favorite game items. For the music lover on your list, make a **Christmas Caroling Bowl of Goodies,** *above,* filled with a book of Christmas carols and all the makings for hot chocolate. To cushion the gift, shred unwanted sheet music. For instructions for all of the gifts, see pages 151–153.

Clever **Christmas Card Coasters**, *above*, are easy to make using last year's Christmas cards and purchased circles of cork. Add a thin ribbon around the edge to finish the coasters. Wrap them in style by topping with a lollipop, cellophane, and a bow. A teacher or other special person will appreciate **Monogrammed Note Cards and Tin**, *opposite*. The purchased tin is decorated using chipboard letters and holds personalized note cards. Instructions are on pages 153–154.

Give a set of simple **Knitted Spa Cloths**, *opposite above*, with a lovely bar
of soap for a pampering gift. The cloths are easy to make using only the knit stitch.
Anyone on your Christmas list will love **Inspirational Spa Pillows**, *opposite below*,
made from soft towels machine stitched and inscribed with a message. Make a set
of **Desk Jar Helpers**, *above*, by covering jar tops with scrapbook papers that
match the jar's contents. Instructions for theses projects are on page 154–156.

Give a little hint about what might be inside your package with **Tell-All Gift Wraps,** *opposite, left and below.* Use a chocolate brown ribbon and a sparkling pin to suggest yummy chocolates inside, *left above.* A velvety stripe of burgundy-colored ribbon hints at a favorite bottle of wine enclosed, *left below.* Wrap gourmet candy canes and give a packet of cocoa mix to match, *opposite below.* Coordinate the motif on some fancy purchased towels with a Christmas trim, *opposite top.* Instructions and ideas are on page 157.

Greeting cards are easy and fun to make using cardstock and other

scrapbook embellishments. Make a set of **Joy Cards** with a special

message inside. Instructions are on page 158.

Merry Christmas Mailbox

Shown on pages 140–141

WHAT YOU NEED

Small tin in shape of mailbox (available at scrapbook and crafts stores)
Acrylic paint in desired color
Paintbrush
Scrapbooking ink (optional)
Patterned scrapbook paper
Cardstock
Decoupage medium
4 small wooden balls
Stickers
Chipboard shapes
Buttons
Ribbon
Circle punch
Embroidery floss
Magnetic tape

HERE'S HOW

1. Paint the mailbox inside and out using desired color of acrylic paint.
2. If desired, rub ink sparingly over paint for distressed look.
3. Trim patterned paper as needed to fit mailbox and adhere using decoupage medium.

4. Punch circles out of coordinating patterned paper and use decoupage medium to adhere to top of mailbox along curve.
5. Coat entire mailbox with two to three coats of decoupage medium.
6. Glue 4 small wooden balls to the bottom of the mailbox.
7. Embellish mailbox as desired using coordinating ribbons and other embellishments such as chipboard, stickers, etc.

Comfort Food Crock with Apron

Shown on page 142

WHAT YOU NEED

Tracing paper; pencil; scissors
1 yard cotton fabric
4½ yards medium (½-inch wide) rickrack
2⅛ yards ⅞-inch-wide red grosgrain ribbon
Matching thread
Large crock bowl
Comfort food

HERE'S HOW

1. To make apron, enlarge and trace pattern, *page 152*. Cut apron and pocket pieces from pattern. Cut ribbon into three 25-inch-long pieces. Set aside.
2. Prepare pockets by stitching ⅜ inch from sides and lower edge. Press edges to wrong side of pocket, just inside of stitching line. Starting 1¼ inches down from top edge, stitch rickrack close to sides and lower edge. Press under ¼ inch on upper edge of pocket to wrong side. Turn upper edge 1 inch over to wrong side again. Stitch rickrack across top of pocket, placing trim ¾ inches down from pocket top fold line and sewing in center of rickrack.
3. Pin pockets to lower part of apron, placing 3½ inches from bottom edge and 3½ inches from center fold. Sew pockets to apron, stitching over the stitching close to the pocket edges, reinforcing at start and finish.
4. To finish armhole edges of apron, press edges ½ inch to wrong side. Turn again ½ inch to wrong side. Place rickrack behind pressed edge and stitch close to the folded edge to stitch in place. Topstitch ⅜ inch from inside finished edge.

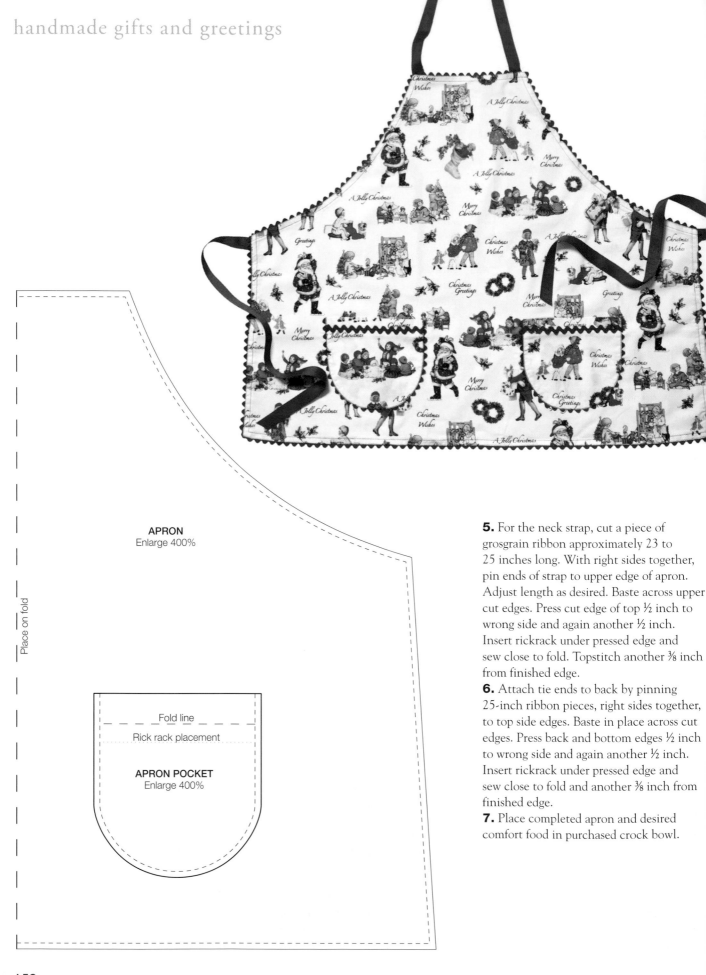

APRON
Enlarge 400%

Place on fold

Fold line

Rick rack placement

APRON POCKET
Enlarge 400%

5. For the neck strap, cut a piece of grosgrain ribbon approximately 23 to 25 inches long. With right sides together, pin ends of strap to upper edge of apron. Adjust length as desired. Baste across upper cut edges. Press cut edge of top ½ inch to wrong side and again another ½ inch. Insert rickrack under pressed edge and sew close to fold. Topstitch another ⅜ inch from finished edge.

6. Attach tie ends to back by pinning 25-inch ribbon pieces, right sides together, to top side edges. Baste in place across cut edges. Press back and bottom edges ½ inch to wrong side and again another ½ inch. Insert rickrack under pressed edge and sew close to fold and another ⅜ inch from finished edge.

7. Place completed apron and desired comfort food in purchased crock bowl.

Fun and Games Box
Shown on page 142

WHAT YOU NEED
Large wrapped box or purchased box
Artificial greenery
Playing cards
Old movies, radio, or other
    entertainment items
Candy
Apples

HERE'S HOW
Arrange the greenery in the bottom of
the box. Add items to the box and pull
greenery up between items for support.

Christmas Caroling Bowl of Goodies
Shown on page 143

WHAT YOU NEED
Large bowl
Christmas caroling book
Hot chocolate mix
Marshmallows in a bag
Mugs; microwave popcorn
Candy canes
Shredded paper made from old
    sheet music

HERE'S HOW
Collect the items to be placed in the
bowl. Feed old printed sheet music
through a paper shredder for the paper
shred. Add remaining items to the bowl.

Christmas Card Coasters
Shown on page 144

WHAT YOU NEED
Christmas cards
4-inch-round cork mats
Glue stick
Strong crafts glue
White crafts glue
Small paintbrush
Pour-on waterproof high-gloss finish
Heavyweight cardboard scraps
Lightweight cardboard scraps
Narrow red ribbon

HERE'S HOW
1. Trace around a cork mat circle onto
lightweight cardboard. Cut circle shape
from center of cardboard to use as a frame
for cutting the cards. Center the cut
circle over Christmas card designs,
choosing the desired location to cut the
circle for the coaster design. Trace around
the circle shape. Using a glue stick adhere
card circle onto the heavyweight
cardboard. After gluing together, cut out
circle from the two layers. Using strong
crafts glue, adhere circle card design onto
the cork mat. Using white crafts glue and
paintbrush, coat coasters with thin layer
of glue to seal all layers. Let dry.
2. Cover work surface. Place coasters on
top of jar lids to elevate them from the
papered work surface. Mix together gloss
finish following directions for product.
Pour thin layer of finish over coasters.
Using paintbrush, coat outside edges with
finish and wipe off any drips running
down the sides of the circle shapes. Cover
coasters with an inverted shoe box to
allow finish to dry free from dust or other
particles for several hours. Finish needs to
totally cure for several days before using.
Any drips on the bottoms can be sanded
off after finish is totally cured.
3. Glue the red ribbon around the edges
of the coaster using white crafts glue.
4. To wrap the coasters, stack and place
the coasters in a cellophane bag. Stand
up a lollipop and tie with ribbon.

Monogrammed Note Cards and Tin

Shown on page 145

For the Tin

WHAT YOU NEED
Tin (see Sources, page 160)
Acrylic paint in desired color
Paintbrush
Scrapbooking ink (optional)
Patterned paper
Die cuts
Decoupage medium
Chipboard letters
Strong crafts glue

HERE'S HOW
1. Paint outside of the tin with acrylic paint. Allow to dry. If desired, ink over paint to tone down paint color.
2. Cover tin with patterned paper and die cuts as desired. Adhere the papers using decoupage medium.
3. To seal the tin, cover entire tin with 1 to 2 coats of decoupage medium.
4. Cover chipboard letters with patterned paper and coat with decoupage medium. Allow to dry. Adhere letters to tin.

For the Note Cards

WHAT YOU NEED
8½×11-inch sheets of cardstock (will yield 2 per sheet)
2×3-inch rectangle of coordinating cardstock
Alphabet letter stamps
Patterned papers
Paper adhesive
Decoupage medium such as Mod Podge

HERE'S HOW
1. Cut each sheet of cardstock in half to 8½×5½ inches. Fold the card in half. Set aside.
2. To create monogram letter, stamp letter onto small cardstock rectangle using lighter color of ink first.
3. Stamp letter a second time using darker ink just to the left of the first image. Note: Use see-through acrylic stamps to make it easier to line up images. Set aside.
4. Complete cards by adhering patterned papers as desired, coordinating papers with gift tin.
5. Adhere stamped letter to front of card.

Knitted Spa Cloths

Shown on page 146

Finished Size: 12×16 inches

WHAT YOU NEED
Classic Elit's Provence, 100% mercerized cotton, DK (double knitting) weight (256 yards per hank): For 4 mats; 2 hands each of Lemon (2612) for Color A and Hydrangea Blossom (2679) for Color B; OR Bright Chartreuse (2681) for Color A and Slate Blue (2648) for Color B
Size 6 (3.75mm) knitting needles or size needed to obtain gauge
Yarn needle

Gauge:
In garter stitch (knit all rows), 20 stitches and 40 rows (20 ridges) = 4"/l0 cm.
Take time to check your gauge.

HERE'S HOW
With A, cast on 60 stitches. Knit all rows changing color at beginning of rows as follows (first row is right side):
12 ridges A, 1 ridge B
8 ridges A, 1 ridge B
6 ridges A, 1 ridge B
4 ridges A, 1 ridge B
2 ridges A, 1 ridge B
1 ridge A, 2 ridges B
1 ridge A, 4 ridges B
1 ridge A, 6 ridges B
1 ridge A, 8 ridges B
1 ridge A, 12 ridges B
Bind off

Finishing: Weave loose ends into wrong side of work.

Inspirational Spa Pillows
Shown on page 146

WHAT YOU NEED
Bolster pillow form
2 hand towels
1½ yard of ⅞-inch-wide grosgrain ribbon
Straight pins; matching thread; scissors
For machine lettering: Satin embroidery
   thread
Tear-away stiffening paper
Water soluable paper such as
   Sulky-Solvy

For hand lettering: Embroidery floss
Wate- soluble marking pen
⅜-inch-wide trim or cording

HERE'S HOW
1. On center of one hand towel, add words by desired method. Words can be stitched with an embroidery sewing machine using decorative threads, stitched by hand using a satin stitch and embroidery floss, or couched on by hand (or machine) using narrow trim or cording and matching thread. Letters can be marked easily on towels or paper with a water-soluble marking pen.
2. *For machine lettering*, mark desired letters or use pattern, *page 156*, on small piece of water soluble paper. Place water soluble paper on top of towel and tear-away paper directly under towel. Use machine-satin stitch to make letter (see Photo A). Continue for all letters. Remove excess water soluble paper. Remove tear away paper from underside of towel (see Photo B). Any remaining water soluble paper will wash out.
3. To hand embroider, mark desired words directly onto towel. Satin stitch, *page 160*, or couch on cording.
4. Using the plain hand towel, wrap towel over bolster pillow horizontally, so that finished short ends of the towel are at side edges of the pillow form. Pin towel to pillow form along long edges, using straight pins.
5. Wrap lettered towel around plain towel, placing long edges across back side of pillow. Hand sew using whip stitch to keep in place.
6. Cut ribbon in half and angle-cut ends. Wrap ribbon around ends of pillow form and tie tightly in a knot or bow, as desired.

A

B

INSPIRATIONAL
SPA PILLOWS
Full-Size Patterns

Calm

PEACE

Desk Jar Helpers
Shown on page 147

WHAT YOU NEED
Small canning jars
Patterned scrapbook papers in colors
   to match contents of jar
Scissors
Pencil
Desk items such as colored rubber
   bands, colored clips, and colored
   paper clips
Crafts glue

HERE'S HOW
Take the top flat off of the canning
jar. Draw around it onto the desired
patterned scrapbook paper. Cut out
and set aside. Fill the jar with desired
items. Place the flat back on the jar and
then the cut circle of scrapbook paper.
Replace the screw top over the flat.
Glue a matching item on top of the
jar. If using rubber bands, make a bow
with the colored rubber bands and
glue in place.

Tell-All Gift Wraps
Shown on pages 148–149

Chocolate Candy Wrap
Wrap favorite candies in a box wrapped with apple green paper and finish with a chocolate-colored ribbon. Pin on a pretty tree pin.

Wine Bottle Wrap
Wrap a wine bottle in tissue paper and slip it into a paper bag that has been trimmed with burgundy-colored velvet ribbon. String brads or make a handle from a beaded necklace.

Candy Cane Wrap
Gourmet candy canes are such a treat. Wrap a few and then add a package of hot chocolate mix to trim the gift.

Towel Motif Wrap
Find a set of pretty towels with a holiday motif for someone on your Christmas list. Then trim the gift with a matching Christmas motif.

Joy Cards
Shown on page 150

For the Noel Card

WHAT YOU NEED
8½×5½-inch piece of
    white cardstock
Scraps of green and brown cardstock
Felt shapes
Die-cut letters
Rub-on phrases

Glitter glue
Tape adhesive
Mini flat glue dots
Paper trimmer
Scoring blade

HERE'S HOW
1. Score and fold white cardstock.
(Card opens on side.)
2. Cut two squares each from green and
brown cardstock. Adhere to front of card
with consistent margins around each.
3. Adhere felt shapes to each square
using mini flat glue dots.
4. Cut "NOEL" using a die-cut system
or use sticker letters or rub-ons. Adhere
to bottom portion of card front using
tape adhesive.
5. Cut a mat for the inside of the card.
Apply "Happy Holidays" rub-on to mat.
6. Add glitter glue to the felt shapes as
desired. Allow to dry before handling.

For the Joy to the World Card

WHAT YOU NEED
11x5½-inch piece of brown cardstock
Scraps of white and red cardstock
Patterned scrapbook paper
Clear tree sticker such as from
    Making Memories

Rub-on letters
Tape adhesive
Paper trimmer
Scoring blade
Scissors
Corner rounder
Small hole punch

HERE'S HOW
1. Score and fold brown cardstock base;
round corners. (Card opens at bottom.)
2. Cut a white cardstock mat for the
front of the card; do not adhere yet.
3. Cut a strip of patterned paper and
adhere down the left side of the white mat.
4. Cut a narrow strip of red cardstock
and adhere to the right edge of the
patterned paper.
5. Apply rub-on letters (Joy to the
World) to the lower right corner of the
white mat.
6. Adhere clear tree sticker to the white
mat, extending off right edge. Trim off
the overhanging portion, then adhere the
completed white mat to the card front.
7. Punch three small red cardstock dots
and adhere to the front of the tree.
8. Print an inside greeting on white
cardstock. Cut out and adhere to inside
of card.

Mailing or Sending Gifts and Greetings
*Here are some things to remember before you take your greeting
cards or gifts to the post office:*

- Square envelopes require extra postage. Check with
  your local post office.
- The thickness of the envelope (with the card inside)
  must be between .007 inch and ¼ inch. Envelopes
  must be between 3½ inches and 6⅛ inches high,
  and between 5 inches and 11½ inches long.
- To make an envelope, use a weight of paper that
  is lighter than cardstock (which is too stiff to fold).
  Avoid glossy and dark papers. The print is difficult to
  read on them, and it is difficult to attach bar codes
  to them.
- To mail dimensional items or small gifts, consider using
  odd-shaped boxes, cans, or other items for the outside
  container. Check with your local post office to find out
  what is acceptable and the applicable charges.

- Because the envelope
  is the "wrap" of your
  greeting card, think of the
  postage stamp as the bow.
  Check the selection of stamps
  and use one with an
  appropriate theme or one that
  coordinates with the color of the envelope.

Special delivery
When the mailing process is not a factor and you decide
to hand-deliver a card or gift, there are more options for
the outer wrap. Try one of these creative items for the wrap
and tie with a ribbon:

Handkerchief	Baby blanket	Scarf
Cellophane	Paper bag	Fabric
Tissue paper	Napkin	Faux leather
Netting	Newspaper	

index

Sources

Candy

Hammond's Candies
hammondscandies.com

Eggs

Handmade Lace Eggs
Lynn Jones
712-539-1457

Hobby Lobby
hobbylobby.com

Michaels
www.michaels.com
1-800-michaels

Ribbon

www.craftopia.com
www.hancockfabrics.com
www.joannfabrics.com
www.jordanpapercrafts.com
www.mayarts.com
www.mjtrim.com
www.papermart.com
www.offray.com
www.midoriribbon.com
www.ribbonlady.com
www.ribbonshop.com

Scrapbooking Supplies

American Craft
www.americancrafts.com

Bazzill
www.bazzillbasics.com

Chipboard Letters:
Basic Grey Chipboard letters
www.basicgrey.com/r

Doodlebug
www.doodlebug.ws

EK Success
www.eksuccess.com

Ki Memories
www.kimemories.com

Making Memories
www.makingmemories.com

Mod Podge
www.plaidonline.com

My Mind's Eye
www.mymindseye.com

Provocraft
www.provocraft.com

QuicKutz
www.quickutz.com

Versamark Archival Ink
www.tsukineko.com

Tips for Felting Wool

"Felting" wool fabric brings the fibers in the wool closer together and gives it a more compact look and feel. The texture becomes more irregular and interesting. Choose 100% wool fabric to felt. Place the wool inside an old pillowcase to prevent any tiny fibers from washing out. Then wash the wool in very hot water with a little laundry detergent. Agitation of the wool loosens fibers and helps to shrink the wool. Dry the wool in a hot dryer to shrink the maximum amount. Press the wool with a press cloth if desired. Tightly felted wool does not ravel and edges and seams can usually be left raw or unfinished similar to purchased felt.

Stitch Diagrams

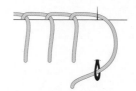

Blanket Stitch

Buttonhole Stitch

Chain Stitch

Fern Stitch

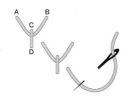

Fly Stitch

Lazy Daisy Stitch

Stem Stitch

Knitting Abbreviations

approx	approximately
beg	begin(ning)(s)
cn	cable needle
dec	decrease(s)(ing)
end	ending
est	established
inc	increase(s)(ing)
k or K	knit
p or P	purl
pat	pattern
pwise	as if to purl
rem	remain(s)(ing)
rep	repeat(s)(ing)
rev	reverse
RS	right side(s) of work
sl	slip
sm	slip marker
st(s)	stitch(es)
St st	stockinette stitch
tbl	through the back loop(s)
tog	together
WS	wrong side(s) of work
yo	yarn over
yon	yarn over needle
yrn	yarn around needle
[ ]	work step in brackets the number of times indicated
( )	work instructions within parentheses in the place directed and the number of times indicated
*	repeat the instructions following the single asterisk as directed